D1567699

MOTOR CITY DREAM GARAGES

AMAZING COLLECTIONS FROM AMERICA'S GREATEST CAR CITY

DISCARDED

IOWA CITY

APR - - 2008

PUBLIC LIBRARY

REX ROY

FOREWORD BY DON SHERMAN

MOTORBOOKS

Dedication

Motor City Dream Garages is dedicated to my father, Ross Roy,
a man who could have had one of the best garages in Detroit.

First published in 2007 by Motorbooks, an imprint of
MBI Publishing Company LLC, Galtier Plaza, Suite 200,
380 Jackson Street, St. Paul, MN 55101 USA

Text copyright © 2007 by Rex Roy
Photos copyright © 2007 by Rex Roy, except where noted

All rights reserved. With the exception of quoting brief
passages for the purposes of review, no part of this
publication may be reproduced without prior written
permission from the Publisher.

The information in this book is true and complete to the
best of our knowledge. All recommendations are made
without any guarantee on the part of the author or
Publisher, who also disclaim any liability incurred in
connection with the use of this data or specific details.

We recognize, further, that some words, model names, and
designations mentioned herein are the property of the
trademark holder. We use them for identification purposes
only. This is not an official publication.

Motorbooks titles are also available at discounts in bulk
quantity for industrial or sales-promotional use. For details
write to Special Sales Manager at MBI Publishing Company,
Galtier Plaza, Suite 200, 380 Jackson Street, St. Paul, MN
55101 USA.

To find out more about our books, join us online at
www.motorbooks.com.

Library of Congress Cataloging-in-Publication Data

Roy, Rex, 1962–
    Motor city dream garages : amazing collections from
america's greatest car city / by Rex Roy ; foreword by Don
Sherman.
        p. cm.
    ISBN-13: 978-0-7603-2989-4 (hardbound w/ jacket)
    1. Garages—Michigan—Detroit Metropolitan Area. 2.
Automobiles—Collectors and collecting—Michigan—
Detroit Metropolitan Area. I. Title.
    TH4960.P49 2007
    629.222074'77434—dc22

                            2007017803

On the cover: Located west of Detroit, Don Soenen's garage
blends old and new in a comfortable space for cars,
motorcycles, and people.

On the frontispiece: Don Soenen leans back in the doorway
of his own Mobilgas service station. Soenen's father is
pictured in the doorway, while Soenen's uncle tends the cash
register. Antique equipment placed "outside" the painted
image helps complete the carefully crafted illusion.

On the title page: A 1916 Ford Model T sits in the center
of the Power House's front garage section. An icon of
industrialization, more than 15,000,000 Model Ts were
produced from 1909 through 1927. The circular pattern of
red tile indicates where the garage's turntable was
originally positioned.

On the back cover, main: The 1934 Chrysler Airflow is
pure art deco with its waterfall grille. Schneider discovered
the porcelain Shell gasoline station façade (background)
behind a false front of a commercial building the couple
owned. **Inset:** Historically significant Mustangs are parked
with retired race cars, show vehicles, and cars that
represent important points in Jack Roush's life and career.
Toward the back of the right row of vehicles is a 1951 Ford
two-door that Roush restored, he says, "as a replacement
for the one I wrecked when I was sixteen [years], six
weeks, and six days old."

Edited by Nicole Edman
Designed by Mandy Iverson

Printed in Hong Kong

TABLE OF CONTENTS

FOREWORD

If you expected his *Motor City Dream Garages* to be glossy coffee-table ballast or yet another paean to every car enthusiast's favorite room, you're in for a surprise. Rex Roy, a friend and colleague for 30 years, goes beyond the usual architectural celebration to pay homage to the world's car capital, the heirs of those who built Detroit, and a few of the milestone automobiles created here. Rex's admiration for the Motor City enables him to look past the expected cozy carriage houses to share insights from the car business you'll never find in *Fortune* magazine. There is no one better suited to guide this tour of the Motor City's finest parking spaces.

One of Rex's insights is how Detroit, of all places, became the twentieth century's dominant automotive force. Before this corner of Michigan devoted its energy to car building, it led the world in several other disciplines. Detroit's first iron foundry was erected in 1820 to cast plowshares. Railways followed before Michigan joined the Union in 1837. Dining, sleeping, and refrigerated-freight cars were all invented here. Bessemer process steel and the first steel rails were made in Detroit in 1864. Thanks to its leadership role in railroads, Detroit was America's center for passenger car manufacturing long before Gottlieb Daimler constructed his automobile prototype. Responding to the need for farm, industrial, and watercraft power, this city began building gasoline engines in the 1880s.

During the last half of the nineteenth century, Detroit entrepreneurs earned fortunes manufacturing paint, varnish, tobacco, pharmaceuticals, chemicals, stoves, shoes, ships, soaps, and seeds. After Bernhard Stroh emigrated from Germany, Detroit became a beer capital. Michigan's mining and lumber tycoons filled local bank accounts with investment capital that would soon be put to profitable use. Before it rolled up its sleeves to build cars, Detroit was considered the loveliest city in America with broad boulevards, ample trees, and cattle grazing in its vacant lots.

While Detroit did not invent the automobile, it quickly taught the world how cars could be manufactured most efficiently. Craftsmanship and enterprise took root and thrived in this city's soul. Today, the automotive tree that grew in Detroit and spread its branches globally is undergoing major pruning. Some of the men who own the garages on these pages face the daunting task of wielding the clippers.

The Roy family began contributing to Detroit's fortunes eight decades ago. "My father, Ross Roy, started out selling Fords in Janesville, Wisconsin," Rex recalls. "After his boss gypped him in a sales contest, he moved to a Dodge Brother's dealership and began striving to gain a leg on the competition.

"His strategy was informing prospects why they should buy a Dodge instead of the other brands they were shopping. A friend who owned an ice cream store helped my father gather facts from all the makers who built delivery trucks. That information was compiled to create what must have been one of the first competitive comparison charts. After my father became the top salesman at his Dodge dealership, others were anxious to discover his secret to success. Ross Roy Incorporated was formed in 1926 when he began traveling city-to-city selling the competitive-comparison literature he published.

"When Chrysler bought Dodge two years later, my father thought he was finished. To the contrary, he was soon summoned to Detroit by a personal telegram from Walter P. Chrysler. In 1981, when my father retired from the advertising agency he created, his business was thriving thanks to its work with Chrysler Corporation, K-Mart, Federal Mogul, La-Z-Boy, and Detroit Bank and Trust."

Rex's car enthusiasm was stimulated by the spanking new Chryslers his father owned. "At ages six or seven, I sat for hours in each of those cars until I'd figured out exactly how everything worked." Rex also inherited his father's entrepreneurial gene. "By the fifth grade, I had a nice business installing stereos and CB radios in cars." He

Photography by Bobby Alcott

spent his teenage summers working in the product information department at his father's agency.

I met Rex in 1979 when he was pursuing extra training at the Bob Bondurant School of High Performance Driving after receiving his driver's license. Rex, 16, and Ross, 81, were both enrolled in the school's anti-terrorist course for chauffeurs because, "my dad and I thought that learning how to do forward and reverse 180s would be a lot of fun."

Rex's first car was a 1973 Dodge Charger powered by a 440 Magnum V-8 handed down from his father. Before his license was six months old, the Magnum V-8, the Bondurant training, and youthful exuberance conspired against Rex. "I was braking from 125 mph on I-94 when I crested a hill and plowed straight into the radar beam of an oncoming trooper," Rex recalls. "I was out of the car, sitting on the trunk with my license and registration in hand before the officer arrived. Luckily, he clocked me at 'only' 97 mph. His first intention was to write me up for reckless driving. But I was so polite that he considered careless driving before downgrading the citation to simple speeding. Still, a ticket for 42 mph over the posted limit triggered a license suspension."

That setback didn't hinder another of Rex's pursuits: spy photography. He soon began bombarding Jean Lindamood (now Jennings) and me with fuzzy shots in hopes of penetrating *Car and Driver*'s editorial pages. To get him out of our hair, we sent him on a goose chase, stalking the front-drive mini-pickup Dodge was developing

for sale in 1982. We were shocked when he bagged his prey while hiding in the bushes at a restaurant near the Chrysler Proving Grounds and snapping away as a couple of engineers driving the undisguised Dodge Rampage prototype munched on lunch.

After a quarter century of building dual careers in marketing and journalism, Rex hasn't lost his knack for hunting down a great story.

—Don Sherman

Don Sherman's byline has seen print in a dozen or more publications during his 36 years as an automotive journalist. After studying engineering at the University of Iowa, the University of Michigan, and the Chrysler Institute of Engineering, Sherman joined Car and Driver *in 1971 as technical editor. Sherman is currently the technical editor at* Automobile Magazine.

Introduction

THE GREATEST GARAGES YOU'LL NEVER SEE

Every town has one or two. Every city has at least a few. Sometimes you catch a glimpse of them cruising on a warm summer evening or heading out to a show early Sunday morning. They're the coolest cars in the neighborhood. Sometimes you recognize familiar shapes like 1932 Fords or 1957 Chevrolets. Other times, you haven't the foggiest notion what you're looking at, and name badges spelling out Kaiser and Cord only remind you of lunch and firewood. But once these cars roll on out of sight, or leave a diner after a cruise night, they head off to unknown parking spaces. They return to the greatest garages you'll never see. Until now.

For the myriad reasons Don Sherman lucidly exposes in this book's Foreword, Detroit is the Motor City, and it only stands to reason that the Detroit area would likely be home to some of the coolest cars and garages on the planet. My town did not disappoint. The sheer number of truly excellent and interesting garages in Detroit and the surrounding communities forced a culling of the ranks.

The *modus operandi* for the selection process was simple: include "Great cars in cool spaces not open to the public." But in order to tell a good story, I broke this hard and fast rule in the first chapter. Of all the garages covered on the following pages, only Henry Ford's Power Station at his Fair Lane Estate is open to the public. The garage's significance outweighed its exclusion. As I learned more about how Henry Ford used his garage at Fair Lane, it became clear that he had much in common with contemporary enthusiasts. In the Power Station, Henry Ford worked on his cars, modified his cars, and displayed his cars. About the only thing that today's enthusiasts do in their garages that old Henry didn't is hang out. Presumably, Henry had the rest of his estate for that, plus those who

knew the man best would not have categorized him as an "enthusiast," so this *failing* can be forgiven.

Precisely because Fair Lane is open to the public, it is one of several important automotive stops in Detroit that should find a place on your itinerary. Two of the world's best automotive museums are also located in the Detroit area: the Henry Ford and the Walter P. Chrysler Museum. Somewhat surprisingly, the Henry Ford is not marque-specific. Staying true to the purpose set forth by the original Henry himself, the Henry Ford includes all manner of transportation within its diverse collection and includes many makes of cars, trucks, planes, and locomotives. Ford Motor Company, while a supporter of the Henry Ford, does not maintain a public or private collection of its own vehicles. The Dearborn manufacturer has essentially left its physical heritage in the hands of the private sector.

Taking a different tack than Ford or Chrysler, General Motors took charge of its vehicular lineage in 2004 with the opening of the General Motors Heritage Collection (Chapter 9). Appropriately the largest of Detroit's Dream Garages, it's not a museum. Vehicles move in and out of the collection to suit the promotional needs of the corporation's various divisions (Cadillac, Pontiac, Buick, etc.). Sometimes utilized for industry gatherings or select GM enthusiast club occasions, the facility meets this book's criteria for inclusion, in that it is not open to the public.

In contrast to GM's tens of thousands of square feet filled with hundreds of cars and trucks, *Motor City Dream Garages* is mostly about private collections. The following chapters profile enthusiasts who have built significant or interesting collections, often located on the same property as their homes. I initially thought it might

Above and previous spread: Located on the grounds of the company's headquarters in Auburn Hills, Michigan, the Walter P. Chrysler Museum chronicles the life of Walter P. Chrysler and the company he started. In addition to featuring traditional Chrysler brands Desoto, Dodge, and Plymouth, the museum also presents the history of the American Motors Corporation (AMC). *Neil Tyson*

take much begging and pleading along with promises of security and even garage-owner anonymity to hit my target of 20 garages. What I encountered was old-fashioned, Midwestern openness and trust. In one garage, the owner needed to leave for a meeting before I had finished the photography. Having only met me 45 minutes earlier, his parting comment was, "Make sure you pull the door shut on your way out." I spent the next three hours photographing $2 million worth of vehicles completely unsupervised. Trust, indeed.

Underscoring this experience is the friendliness of Detroit's car community. There is not a single snob among the garage owners profiled here. They like their cars and trucks, and they gladly welcome others with the same interests. These people have opened their private space to you, and they have trusted me to bring you their personal stories and those of their collections. I hope you enjoy the experience.

—Rex Roy

Located on 90 acres in Dearborn, Michigan, the Henry Ford and Greenfield Village comprise one of America's greatest historical attrations. Displays often put items in context, helping bring American ideas and innovations to life. *Photos courtesy of the Henry Ford*

Chapter 1
THE FIRST DREAM GARAGE

GARAGE OWNER: **HENRY FORD**

Photography by Rex Roy and courtesy of University of Michigan, Dearborn

There had to be one. The first. Not a converted stable. Nor a modified barn or garden shed. But a purpose-built space designed expressly for the enjoyment, display, and maintenance of automobiles. Perhaps this is it—Henry Ford's Power House.

This exciting and significant building is integral to the first famous Ford's magnificent Fair Lane Estate in Dearborn, Michigan. Constructed between 1914 and 1915, the four-story structure gets its name from the fact that it was, and still is, a working hydro-powered electrical generation station. Pittsburg architect William Van Tine designed the limestone structure, but no doubt received engineering advice from Henry Ford's good friend, Thomas Edison. It was Edison, in fact, who laid the cornerstone for the building. Fittingly, the cornerstone is positioned just above the sluice that directs rushing water from the Rouge River toward hydro turbines on a lower level of the structure.

Upper levels of the Power House include the actual dynamos that produce electricity used at the estate, plus the transformers and additional gear needed to convert the generated direct current (DC) power into alternating current (AC). Still today, the Power House provides for the needs of Fair Lane and pumps electricity back into the regional power grid.

The west, or riverside, portion of the building is all about generating power of an electrical kind. The east side of the building is all about automotive power. Large enough to accommodate twelve vehicles, the garage features many custom touches designed and engineered expressly for the use and enjoyment of automobiles.

Five garage doors provide access to the building from the original brick-paved courtyard. The glass-paneled

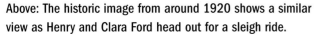

Above: The historic image from around 1920 shows a similar view as Henry and Clara Ford head out for a sleigh ride.

Previous spread: The Power House is the garage of Henry Ford's Fair Lane Estate in Dearborn, Michigan. This easterly view shows five garage doors that open to the original brick courtyard.

Viewed from the west, the multiple stories of the Power House follow the terraced bank of the Rouge River. Openings for the tailraces are visible, and provide an exit for the river water used to turn the generators that still produce power for the estate.

garage doors and large windows on the adjoining sides provide plenty of natural light. The garage's glazed-tile floor and walls highlight the practicality of the space, as does the center area where an auto turntable once was.

Records indicate that in addition to owning their namesake products, the Fords drove or were chauffeured in cars by Rolls Royce, Mercedes, Mercer, Marmon, and Cadillac. These were large, luxurious cars that did not yet benefit from power steering—it hadn't yet been invented. The 18-foot turntable, manufactured by the Canton Foundry & Machine Co., once spun these grand cars into position with the greatest of ease. The cars would be driven straight into the garage and onto the turntable. Once on the platter, the car could be rotated by hand, a process so easy a child could do it because of the low-friction ball-bearing mechanism. Once "aimed" toward its assigned parking space, the car would simply drive off the turntable and into its slot. When the estate was decommissioned as a home in 1951, the turntable was removed. The center area also has an in-floor drain and a wash rack that once came down from the ceiling.

Occupying center stage today is the historically significant 1916 Model T fitted with a five-passenger touring body. This automobile represents the 15 million Model Ts produced between 1909 and 1927. The Model T put the motorcar within financial reach of average Americans and made travel on the country's early roads plausible thanks to its high ground clearance and use of high-strength vanadium steel for durability. Without question, the Model T stands as the most significant car ever produced.

The Power House holds another Model T, a 1920 edition that was Ford's personal car. It served as a rolling test lab for new parts and engineering concepts, such as the nickel-plated radiator.

Much is known about Mr. Ford's reticence to embrace change, so it is no surprise that he was slow to take a Model A as his personal car. Mr. Ford's Model A is a 1929 model, but the new design was launched in December 1927. Ford's personal car incorporates features such as experimental brake drums, special upholstery, cowl vents, and a built-in holder for ever-present bottles of Poland Mineral Water, something Mr. Ford always had on hand. This feature may be the original ancestor to the modern cup holder.

Parked next to the Model A is a truck that foreshadows another automotive trend. An argument could be made that this 1922 Lincoln truck is the world's first sport utility recreational vehicle. Mr. Ford loved the outdoors and, along with notables including Thomas Edison, John Burroughs (American naturalist), and Harvey Firestone (of tire manufacturing fame), Ford would embark on camping trips in northern Michigan and across the country. The Lincoln transported camping equipment and support personnel on some of "The Vagabond's" last trips. Burroughs passed in 1921, but Ford, Edison, and

Firestone "camped" until 1923.

The newest vehicle in the Power House is Mr. Ford's 1942 V-8 sedan. It has the ignominious distinction of being the car Ford rode in on the day he died, April 7, 1947.

Brass-trimmed electricity outlets are purposefully placed along the Power House garage's north wall. These DC outlets recharged Mrs. Clara Ford's Detroit Electric Model 47 Brougham, and the electric cars driven by friends and business associates who visited the estate. Mrs. Ford's Detroit Electric is not part of today's Fair Lane collection. In its stead is a similar model owned by the wife of Henry Joy, president of the Packard Motor Car

A 1916 Ford Model T sits in the center of the Power House's front garage section. An icon of industrialization, more than 15,000,000 Model Ts were produced from 1909 through 1927. The circular pattern of red tile indicates where the garage's turntable was originally positioned.

Company. This simple example historically demonstrates the popularity of electric vehicles among well-to-do women shortly after the turn of the century. (See chapter 11 on Jim Cousens' garage for more on electric cars.)

A hydro-powered elevator transported vehicles and equipment between floors. It was surely well used shuttling prototypes from the development laboratories on the top floor to the main garage. Working in these labs, Mr. Ford and his engineers developed the Fordson tractor line plus innovations that later debuted on production Model T and Model A vehicles.

An unrestored 1920 Model F tractor occupies a space where Ford himself probably fabricated prototypes of what came to be known as the "Model T of the Soil." These inex-

The upper floors of the Power House were used as laboratories and engineering test labs. Ideas that Ford and his engineers conceived could be designed, developed, and installed on-site.

The 1929 Model A and the 1942 V-8 sedan were Mr. Ford's last two personal vehicles. Both were also modified over the course of their lives. The Model A is fitted with a bottle holder for the Poland Mineral Water Ford preferred. The V-8 sedan utilized experimental soy-based plastics.

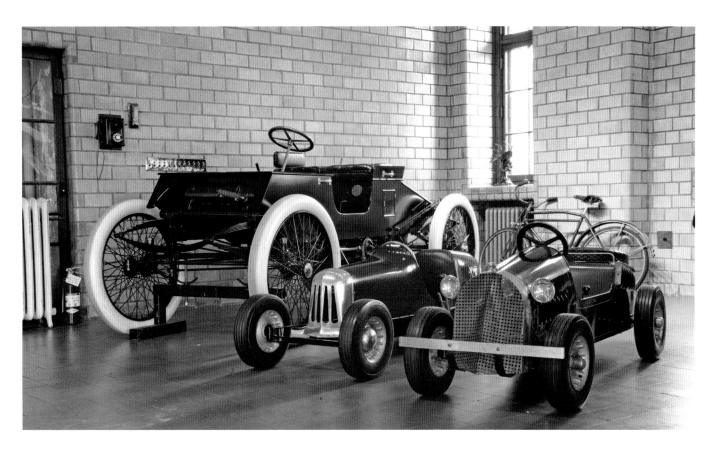

The Ford grandchildren enjoyed scaled-down gasoline-powered cars made by Custer Specialty Company. Parked behind these little raceabouts is one of the earliest known race cars, the 1901 Sweepstakes. Its win at a horse racing track in Grosse Pointe, Michigan, helped Mr. Ford secure financing for one of his early automotive businesses.

pensive tractors sold at annual rates as high as 100,000 units. They certainly helped enable America's huge agricultural boom and the success of the iconic family farm throughout the first half of the twentieth century. The Fordson in the garage today has come full circle. It was first given to Mrs. Ford's brother, H. H. Bryant, a Ford dealer and part-time rancher living in Idaho. Bryant used the tractor for decades. The Bryant family donated the still operational tractor to the collection at the close of the 1980s.

In addition to using the Power House for engineering development work, Mr. Ford parked his family's recreational vehicles and his first automotive creation, the 1896 Quadricycle, in the garage. The Quadricycle now on display is a replica of Mr. Ford's original, which is on display nearby at the Henry Ford Museum. Cars for Clara and Henry's grandchildren were also stored and maintained in the Power House. Custer Specialty Company manufactured these scaled-down gasoline-powered cars. The Ford grandchildren drove them extensively on the expansive road system of the estate. The Fords even kept their sleigh in the garage, a Portland Cutter produced in 1900.

A recent addition to the garage is known simply as Sweepstakes. It is one of the world's oldest race cars, being built in 1901 by Henry Ford, Oliver Barthel, and Ed Huff. Displacing an enormous 8.8 liters from only two pistons (each 7 inches in diameter), the engine produced an estimated 26 horsepower that reportedly propelled Sweepstakes to a fear-inducing 72 miles per hour. To put this speed into perspective, remember that there were no paved roads to drive on, and that the steering and suspension systems of the time were only marginally improved over those of horse-drawn buggies. While Sweepstakes was equipped with a brake, its performance was merely suggestive.

Henry Ford put America on wheels and American family farms in business. The Model T revolutionized automobiles, while the Fordson Model F brought mechanized power to the nation's breadbasket.

Above and opposite: The 1896 Quadricycle was Henry Ford's first "car." This rear view shows the complexity of this primitive automobile. As shown in the archival photograph taken in the Power House around 1932, Ford kept the car on display. In the opposite image, he is pointing out a feature to his wife, Clara.

Piloting such a machine required pure drive and fearlessness.

Ford used Sweepstakes to challenge an already successful auto manufacturer, Alexander Winton. The duo dueled at a horseracing track in Grosse Pointe, Michigan.

Ford won the race handily, a victory that helped secure financing for the Henry Ford Company. Ford left that company in 1903 after a disagreement with his financiers and then founded the Ford Motor Company.

Sweepstakes was sold in 1902 to help the entrepreneur's cash flow, but Mr. Ford repurchased the car in the 1930s. The original body had been destroyed in a fire, but Ford restored the car to its original design and later placed it in his museum. Over time, the museum's staff began to believe that the car was not the original Sweepstakes, but one of two replicas built during the intervening decades. Only with the excitement surrounding Ford Motor Company's 100th anniversary did careful examination of Sweepstakes reveal it to be the original car.

According to University of Michigan, Dearborn, professor Frank Gasiorek, the Power House cost approximately $244,000 in 1915, the equivalent of nearly $5,000,000 today. "The building stands as evidence of

Mr. Ford's prosperity, ingenuity, and resourcefulness," Gasiorek states. He went on to explain that several of the garage's features were adopted by Edsel Ford, son of Henry and Clara, when he designed the garage for his own estate.

As Edsel came of age and married, he left Fair Lane and built his own estate to enjoy with his wife, Eleanor. Their home, completed in 1929, still stands on the shores of Lake St. Clair in Grosse Pointe, just northeast of Detroit. While the English Cotswold style of the home and its massive Gate Lodge are completely different from Fair Lane, the young Edsel clearly appreciated features incorporated into his father's garage. Edsel's carriage house features similar interior materials and a turntable that is still in place.

Edsel died well before his time (he was only 49 years old when he passed away in 1943). His widow lived in their home until she died in 1976. A trust fund continues to preserve the estate for the benefit of the public, and like Fair Lane, it is open for tours.

The garage is included in tours, and houses two vehicles that are personally relevant to the second generation of Fords: Edsel's 1941 Lincoln Continental Cabriolet (a

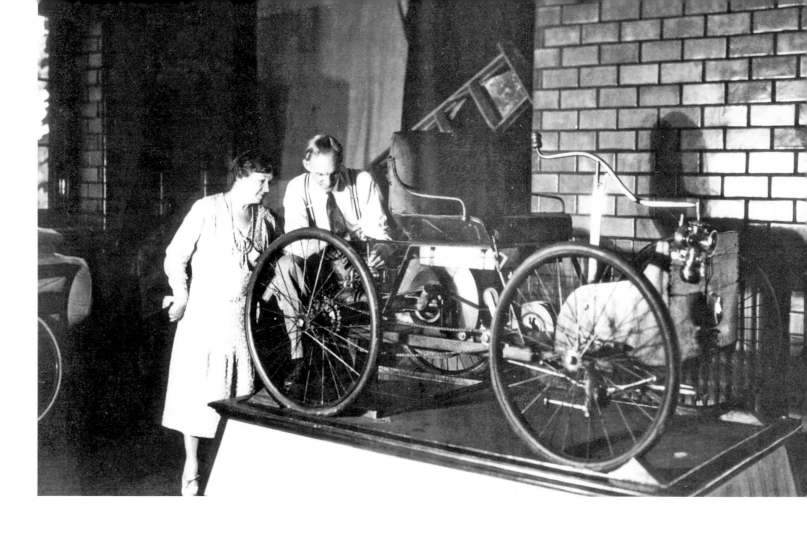

Below: Mrs. Ford preferred to drive an electric vehicle. This car, on loan to Fair Lane from the Detroit Historical Museum, is nearly identical to her 1914 Detroit Electric and dwarfs Ford's 1896 Quadricycle.

Left: Two of Edsel Ford's children routinely lapped the driveways of the Fair Lane estate in these gasoline-powered toy cars made by Custer Specialty Company. Photographed in 1934 are Henry Ford's grandchildren, Josephine and William Clay (the current owner of the Detroit Lions).

Right: Ford's 1922 Lincoln truck was a forerunner of today's SUVs and RVs. He used the vehicle on camping trips. Always health conscious, Ford traveled with bottled water from Maine. Note the refrigerator mounted inside the truck's cargo area.

Left: Edsel Ford said, "Father makes the most popular car in the world. I would like to make the best car in the world: Lincoln." He nearly achieved his goal with his 1940–1948 Lincoln Continental (left), a car he commissioned after visiting Europe and seeing the work of the Continent's finest coachbuilders. A scale model of the 1940 continental shows the pure lines of the original concept by Chief of Ford Design Bob Gregorie. Eleanor Ford's 1952 Lincoln Town Car (right) is heavily modified to obtain a look reminiscent of classic phaetons. Mrs. Ford frequently used the car, as its odometer shows more than 92,000 miles.

Built just off Grosse Pointe's Lake Shore Road, Edsel Ford's Gate Lodge is a combination estate entrance, eight-car garage, and staff quarters.

The garage entrance to Edsel's Gate Lodge is made via a motor court on the structure's north side. Thick wood doors roll open to reveal a spacious interior with vaulted ceilings. Edsel's personal 1941 Continental Cabriolet is parked on the garage's turntable.

vehicle design he championed) and Eleanor's rebodied 1952 Lincoln Town Car. Even though Mrs. Ford appreciated her husband's sense of style regarding automobiles, one look at the unfortunate design of her Lincoln Town Car shows that little of his style rubbed off.

Just as Henry Ford's Power House influenced his son's garage, features and design characteristics seen in the structure continue to have an effect on those designing modern dream garages. Abundant evidence appears on the following pages.

While no exhaustive scholarly research has determined incontrovertibly that Henry Ford's garage is, in fact, the very first purpose-built dream garage in Detroit, an older structure fitting this author's criteria has yet to reveal itself. Until such time, the Power House at Fair Lane holds that distinction. ◆

EDSEL FORD II—THE CURRENT GENERATION

Edsel Ford II, great-grandson of the original Henry, lives in Grosse Pointe, Michigan. His Dutch Reform–style home sits just a few miles from where his father (Henry Ford II) and his grandfather (Edsel) once resided. With estates the size of his namesake's currently out of fashion, Edsel II favors a more modest domicile.

The still generously sized home features two garages connected by an arch over the home's driveway, a feature similar to the arch over the main entrance to the original Edsel's estate. In a manner that typified Edsel II's practical and low-key approach to life, he says, "The garage is a strictly utilitarian space where I store my cars." Apparently, his home provides more elegant and comfortable areas for socializing.

About his cars, Edsel II matter of factly states, "I only have cars that I love to drive or look at." His collection proves his words true and includes a 1970 Jaguar Mark II, a 1971 Ferrari Daytona Spyder, and a 1996 Aston Martin DB-7. His two newest sports cars include a 2005 Ford GT and a 2006 Shelby FIA Cobra. Our interview occurred during the depths of winter, and he apologized that most of his cars were "away at camp for the season." During warmer months, all of the cars are accommodated in his available garage space.

Regardless of the weather, Edsel II always keeps one of his special vehicles close at hand, and this one doesn't mind the snow. His pride in his 1966 Bronco figuratively pours out of this urbane Harvard-educated man. He lights up when he talks about the restoration process he put the SUV through, and how his Ford-blue truck responds to the accelerator. Edsel II says, "It has a crate engine from Ford Racing, so this thing really moves out when you hit the throttle." The Bronco is a common site on the streets of Grosse Pointe, as is Edsel II.

The son of Henry Ford II, and great grandson of the original Henry, Edsel Ford II is retired from Ford Motor Company, but retains a position on the board. His taste in cars runs the gamut from his stunning Ferrari Daytona Spyder to his first-generation Ford Bronco.

This 1966 Ford Bronco occupies valuable real estate inside Edsel Ford II's seven bays of garage space. Lurking under the stock-looking façade is a high-horsepower crate engine supplied by Ford Racing. The garage space is sparse, reflecting this Ford's utilitarian views—and the fact that he doesn't do his own wrenching.

Chapter 2
MAXIMUM BOB'S CAR PARK

GARAGE OWNER: **ROBERT LUTZ**

Photography by John Martin

Anybody who knows anything about the automobile business knows about Bob Lutz. If you don't, here's your chance to get caught up on one of the most influential guys in the biz and see inside his great garage.

Today, Lutz is General Motors' vice chairman of global product development. With that title, the buck stops with him when it comes to all new car programs. Recent new vehicles bearing his approving signature include the sporty Pontiac Solstice and the returning Chevrolet Camaro due in 2008.

Prior to his important work at the General, Lutz championed Chrysler's original 1989 Dodge Viper concept. At the close of the '80s, Chrysler's product line was staler than month-old bagels. Lutz's concept and the production roadster that followed in 1992 energized the company and helped Chrysler become known as the only domestic manufacturer with design guts and daring engineering.

These two career highlights don't even scratch the surface of Lutz's 40-plus years in the business (he's in his mid-70s now), but they do point to a person who systemically knows about cars. He loves cars with an intelligent and enthusiastic passion. His dream garage proves that.

Lutz keeps his cars at his home in Ann Arbor, just 45 minutes due west of Detroit. Situated on more than 100 wooded acres, the Lutz Farm is a private place far removed from the nonstop hustle and politics that typify executive life at a major auto manufacturer.

The compound entrance is a modest-looking driveway set off a country two-lane. There are no ornate gates or fancy Corinthian columns. That would be gauche to Lutz, a man who clearly favors the modest over the ostentatious. Off the public road, a thin asphalt ribbon winds up and around a hill and past a large pond.

The first thing you notice past the pond is the helicopter parked in the driveway. Lutz flew whirly birds in the Marines and often uses his own craft to slice his commute time to GM facilities in the area. Continuing on this aeronautical note, the retired USMC captain eschews golf

Previous spread: Tucked away down a quaint gravel drive sits Bob's Garage. It's a simple building that houses six of Lutz's 16 cars and trucks. Not included in this count are the helicopter, jet fighter, or numerous motorcycles.

Bob Lutz's home is located west of metro Detroit in the college town of Ann Arbor. The estate sits on 147 wooded acres and features gently rolling hills.

Captain Robert A. Lutz, USMC (retired), still looks ready for active duty. His easy, relaxed manner leads to great storytelling and an almost endless knowledge of all things automotive.

Lutz is constantly in motion; buffing, adjusting, tinkering, and dragging on a cigar. Here, he is wiping down his 1953 Cunningham C3 Vignale coupe. Lutz explained that Briggs Cunningham built the road-going version of his racer to maintain his eligibility to race at Le Mans.

as a hobby in favor of flying jets. Located just east of his home is Willow Run airport where he houses his fighter, a Cold War–era Czech-made Albatross military trainer.

Behind the copter is a Swiss-style chalet nestled into mature trees. Given Lutz's continental heritage, the style seems completely appropriate. One could easily imagine a farm family living on the second floor while the livestock and farm implements occupied the first. This structure is the guesthouse, with the main residence being a short distance away. Our destination was the property's third building, a modest wood-faced structure. Bob's Garage.

One might think that Lutz's executive secretary would have delegated the task of prepping Bob's cars for this interview. Certainly, executives like Lutz have minions at

This Cunningham C4R competed at Le Mans in 1954 and placed well. Under the aluminum hood sits a Chrysler Hemi fed by four downdraft Weber carburetors. Behind the C4R is a 1952 Aston Martin DB2 Vantage once owned by Lutz's father. Lutz found and restored the car some 50 years after his father owned it.

Captivated by its advanced engineering, Lutz knows all the details of his 1934 Riley MPH sports racer. A rare survivor of only a handful originally built, the aluminum body is hung over an ash frame. Clever engineering features abound, including a sequential semi-automatic gearbox and adjustable brakes featuring massive 18-inch magnesium drums.

their disposal, but Bob takes care of his own cars, thank you. As we approached the garage, Bob was there, towel in hand wiping down his Cobra.

Bob's garage contains a small assembly as diverse as the man himself, including a 1985 Autocraft Cobra, a 1952 Aston Martin DB2 Vantage, a 1934 Riley MPH, a 1952 Cunningham C4R, a 1953 Cunningham C3 Vignale coupe, and a 1976 Steyr Pinzgauer Swiss military vehicle. As a genuine car guy would, Lutz had reasons for owning each and every one.

"The Aston was actually my father's car. I found it in a rather desolate state, but then I located the factory build ticket and had it restored to exactly the way my father had it," Lutz recounts. With a laugh in his voice, Lutz continues, "When I reunited my father with his car after 55 years,

which he loved when he had it, he said, 'Why would you pay all this money to buy my car back?'"

The rationale for owning the beautiful Vignale-bodied Cunningham C3 seemed downright reasonable, "I always wanted a C3, from the time I was a kid. To me, they were always more desirable than Ferraris. They went faster, were bigger, and you could see yourself being able to afford the maintenance. Where Ferraris are now quite exotic, back then they were really problem cars to own. Nobody could fix them and they broke often." Lutz knew that the C3's Chrysler Hemi was as reliable as it was powerful, making the choice of the Cunningham over the Ferrari simply sensible.

Speaking generally about his collection, Lutz says, "I'm not the kind of guy to buy a million dollar car and sit on it for two or three years and hope to sell it for two million. My collection

Lutz is Swiss. He spent some great years at Chrysler. This combination makes this 1972 Monteverdi 375 High Speed a perfect fit in Lutz's collection. Powered by a 440-cubic-inch V-8 originally supplied by Chrysler, the car sports the look of an Italian exotic but was conceived and built by the Swiss manufacturer Peter Monteverdi.

Lutz points out the six-cylinder engine in his 1934 Citroen 15/6 Traction Avant. This rare fitment sets his car apart from the tens of thousands of four-cylinder models. The body is by the American producer Budd, and was among the first generation of unitized automotive body/frame structures.

is made up of all relatively inexpensive cars that I have because I like them. And I drive them all." Lutz is a familiar face at major road rallies in California, New Mexico, Arizona, and Colorado.

And Lutz doesn't just drive them, he knows about and appreciates every detail of each one of his cars. His C3 has its original bumpers, which he surmises are from a '40s vintage Plymouth—minus a chunk removed from the middle to make them the appropriate width for the Ferrari-sized body. His Riley sports on-the-fly adjustable front/rear brake bias and a primitive but effective sequential gearbox (circa 1934). His knowledge is encyclopedic, born of genuine passion and a strong mind that effortlessly places each vehicle in its historical and current context.

Beyond the cars in the memorabilia-filled main garage, his guesthouse and main residence also have garages. He was admittedly a bit reticent to reveal their contents, but persistence paid off. Nearly the entire first floor of the guesthouse chalet is garage space. Crowded garage space. One area is reserved for Lutz's ever-updated collection of superbikes. Pick the latest, highest horsepower, best handling, and most technically sophisticated motorcycles on the planet, and Bob probably has one here or at his other home in Switzerland. Lutz's still Marine-like physique makes it easy to imagine this near octogenarian donning leathers and swinging a leg over

the saddle of one of these two-wheeled rockets for a blast through the Alps.

Lutz's 1955 Chrysler C300 is parked in the same garage as the bikes. Outfitted for long-distance historic road rallies, the 4-inch-wide racing belts don't seem out of place. Enjoying telling a story about the old red Chrysler, Lutz says, "It looks completely stock, but it's got adjustable Koni shocks, 14-inch Corvette brakes, and in place of the old two-speed automatic, a heavy-duty three-speed TorqueFlite transmission out of a Dodge Ram pickup. It also has very big sway bars. In the hills outside of Eureka, California, during the California Mille, the 300 would easily chase down old Porsches through the canyons. It would scare the hell out of them charging up in their rearview mirrors in a four-wheel drift!"

Stories like this flowed freely, as each garage occupant had his or her own story. Lutz talked on about his 1978 Little Red Express pickup by Dodge, the second production Viper ever made, his six-cylinder Citroen 15/6 Traction Avant, a Chrysler-powered 1972 Monteverdi 375 High Speed, and a 1934 LaSalle convertible—a car Lutz owns because it is similar to the very first automobile he remembers as a child.

As the doors of each garage closed, it was more than obvious why Mr. Robert Lutz is a powerhouse in the automotive business. His passion rings true, and shows so clearly in his own dream garage. ◆

Chapter 3
THE BIG RED BARN

GARAGE OWNER: **CHUCK & DIANE SCHNEIDER**

Photography by Bobby Alcott & Rex Roy

From 1910 to 2005, a big red barn located in Hadley, Michigan, was just that—a traditional working barn. "When we bought the property in 2005," says Chuck Schneider, "the floors were dirt and there was hay upstairs." After a solid year of work, the transformation is remarkable.

Chuck's wife, Diane, adds, "We figuratively dropped off the face of the earth to do the barn. We didn't make it to the 2006 Barrett Jackson auction in Phoenix. It was the first time we've missed in 15 years. Our car collecting friends thought we had cancer or were getting a divorce." As the word gets out on what the Schneiders have created about a 90-minute drive north of Detroit, the couple's friends will understand what the pair has been up to.

A little background: Chuck and Diane met at a car show in 1992, a good omen and clear foreshadowing of their future. Diane, or "Flipper" as her car friends know her, was showing her Estee Lauder "Faultless Fuchsia" (a lipstick color) 1932 Ford V-8 hot rod. She and her father built the car, and over the years she has put more than 70,000 miles on it.

As they quickly realized, their meeting was destiny. Chuck and Diane were deeply entrenched in Detroit's automotive culture, Chuck as a senior executive at Ford Motor Company and Diane as an integral member of the Chevrolet team at the legendary Campbell-Ewald advertising agency. Not long into the marriage, they made a success out of a bed and breakfast that they purchased. This endeavor gave the pair a chance to exercise their love of collecting. Each guest room at their retreat featured a different theme; one was an antique barbershop, another a beauty shop, and yet another a bank.

Walking in the barn's main entrance, one is greeted by a 1946 Hudson pickup. Compared to other trucks of the era, the Hudson was smooth and modern. Behind the truck is an original Hudson dealership sign. Neon is an integral part of the Schneiders' collection and is visible from every angle.

Previous spread: Chuck and Diane Schneider purchased this working farm in 2005 and immediately set to transforming the circa 1910 round-roof barn to house their collection of streamlined collectibles.

Representing the 1950s is a perfect 1957 Dodge Sweptside D100. This truck is a custom creation from the factory, featuring the finned rear fenders used on Dodge sedans.

Chuck Schneider loves streamlined styling. This is evident even in his choice of pickups. This 1937 Hudson Terraplane long-wheelbase Big Boy features full skirts covering the rear wheels.

And then the car collecting started. Chuck notes, "I'm strictly driven by styling. I particularly like the Airflow period," referencing his perfect 1934 Chrysler Airflow sedan, a quintessential art deco design. "Everything I have reflects that I like things streamlined, period. As far as American cars go, the Airflow is streamlined, as are my trucks and the Cadillac. Of course, the Delage is too, but it's French. Even my tractors are streamlined."

The collection the Schneiders have assembled reflects Chuck's focus. And the wide variety of vehicles is displayed in a setting that is truly *unique* in the dictionary definition of the term.

"Based on our research, we think the barn was built around 1910," Diane says. "It's a round-roof barn, which is pretty rare compared to the more common hip-roof design." The pair had specific ideas for what the barn could become and set out to make it work for them after purchasing the property. They built onto the barn's backside, tripling

A rare 1937 Studebaker Coupe Express pickup shares floor space with three true classics, a 1940 Fleetwood Convertible Coupe, a 1935 Delage D8 85 featuring a one-off body by Clabot, and a 1934 Chrysler Airflow.

the structure's square footage. Diane continues, "We hired Amish craftsmen from a town north of here to raise the ceiling for us because we wanted enough room to display all of our neon."

"We wanted a place where everybody would be comfortable and have something to interest them," says Chuck. "All of this is interesting to people, especially those who aren't into cars." The couple often entertains groups, including car, tractor, and travel trailer enthusiast clubs.

Walking in the barn's main pedestrian entry, your eyes adjust to the neon glow to reveal two unusual pickup trucks. One is a rare 1946 Hudson. Chuck walked around the

pickup explaining his approach to acquisitions, "I don't tend to buy my cars at auction because I just like the personal touch of knowing the owner and learning the history of the owner and the car. For instance, this one came from a flour mill in Pennsylvania. One of its employees bought it, and then I bought it from him." Schneider further explained that Hudson was one of the first companies to revamp its product line after World War II, so this truck was an all-new design in 1946. From the B-pillar forward, it matches same-year Hudson sedans. From the cab back, it's pure pickup.

One can see where the '46 Hudson got its good looks. A 1938 Hudson Terraplane pickup is parked alongside it.

This "Big Boy" is one of two known to exist and is special due to its long wheelbase and box configuration. Schneider explains, "This was designed to ferry workers to and from work sites, and they sat on the built-in benches that make up the walls of the bed."

Just a year older than the Terraplane, a bright red 1937 Studebaker Coupe Express shows what another manufacturer thought a pickup could be. The design stands out with details such as a tucked and rolled rear bed and curved tailgate.

Representing the 1950s in Schneider's collection of pickups is another rare find, a 1957 Dodge Sweptside D100. This pickup could easily be considered the antithesis of a typical work truck. The Sweptside was an ultra-luxurious and stylish truck for its day, featuring lots of chrome, finned rear fenders from a Dodge sedan, and a wood-lined cargo box. These trucks were literally hand-built by the Dodge Special Equipment Group (SEG). This group was responsible for adding special equipment to production vehicles bought by Dodge's biggest fleet customers. But, in this rare case, the SEG helped the division take on the popular Chevrolet Cameo (a competitive highline pickup) by customizing standard Dodge D100s. While the overall look is pure '50s Americana, a closer look reveals how crudely some aspects of the conversion were completed. The finned fenders don't really line up with the bed very well, and the tailgate is more like what you'd find on a station wagon than a truck.

The Sweptside, with its posh interior with pushbutton transmission shifting, is faithfully restored to as-new condition. The only deviation from stock is under the hood. Where there was once a 315-cubic-inch Poly Dome V-8, Schneider opted to install a more powerful 392-cubic-inch Hemi that would have originally powered a Chrysler Imperial or New Yorker. Chuck likes the sound of the bigger Hemi.

All of these trucks fit Schneider's "streamlined" requirement, but none are as elegant as the cars parked in the barn. One of Schneider's favorites is the 1934 Chrysler Airflow. With its elegant waterfall grille and three-bar bumper arrangement, the art deco creation from Detroit is immediately recognizable. Distinctive touches such as the winged hood ornament are simply beautiful to study. While it's a clear styling statement, Schneider also admires the car because it is a triumph of engineering. The car was the first automobile known to have been tested in a wind tunnel.

Frivolous features show off the custom styling touches from the Clabot house of design. This unique creation was featured at Delage's 2005 Pebble Beach Concours D'Elegance for the 100th anniversary.

Chuck and Diane Schneider met at a car show. Chuck spent his career at Ford Motor Company, and Diane's career included milestones such as being the first female automotive dealership sales manager in the Metro Detroit area.

This unrestored tractor was built in Benton Harbor, Michigan, around 1930. The tractor is made of cast iron and has survived well. The tractor's bug-like face is unmistakable and a bit intimidating.

As the story goes, Chrysler engineers contracted the testing to none other than Wilbur Wright, and the car's smooth styling reflects Wright's research. The Airflow was the first automobile to utilize an all-steel unit body, and to position the engine above the front axle. These characteristics vastly improved the car's ride, handling, and safety. With only a small six-cylinder engine, Airflows could easily cruise more than at 70 mph. With the larger eight-cylinder engines found in Chrysler models (as opposed to the more economy-minded Desoto models), top speeds approached 100 mph.

Schneider's Cadillac is one of only 14 ever produced. It is a 1940 Fleetwood Convertible Coupe built on a limousine-like 141-inch wheelbase. This national award winner balances its enormous size with smooth lines penned by the General Motors Art and Colour Studio under the direction of

Harley Earl. While there are jump seats in the rear section of the cockpit, it is designed as a two-seater.

The zenith of the Schneiders' collection is the 1935 Delage D8 85. During the classic era of motorcars, manufacturers such as Delage would produce a rolling chassis complete with an engine. The car buyer would then select a coachbuilder to create a body (familiar American coach builders include LeBaron, Locke, Brunn, and Fleetwood). Sometimes bodies were standardized in limited production runs, but at other times, a truly unique creation was built. Records indicate that this Delage chassis was originally fitted with a body from Chaprone.

The car surprisingly survived World War II. Shortly after the Allied victory, the car resurfaced and for some reason was rebodied, a common practice for owners of premium-chassis cars. The new body came from the French masters at Clabot. Chuck Schneider describes his Delage: "This is kind of over the top. I call it Gaudy Deco. The dorsal fin on the rear deck serves no purpose, but it sure looks great. The detailing on the car is terrific. If you look closely, you can see similarities in the design of the hood and grille with those of several American cars such as the Cord 812. There's even a hint of shark nose Graham."

The Schneiders were invited to display their Delage at the 2005 Pebble Beach Concours d'Elegance. The marque was celebrating its one hundredth anniversary, and the couple's D8 85 acquitted itself quite well. Though the vehicle didn't place, Diane recalls, "We know how political the judging is at major concours, and we didn't go expecting to win. We were glad to be there and to be a part of the excitement."

The fact that the barn houses the Delage and several farm tractors may seem to be a complete contradiction. The Schneiders are not schizophrenic. Their tractors, when looked at in context, dramatically expand the collection's scope while staying true to Chuck Schneider's affinity for streamlined designs.

Chuck starts his walk through his tractors with a scary looking machine resting on wheel dollies (its tires are flat). Wearing an unrestored finish of iron oxide, this vintage Kaywood tractor was manufactured in Benton Harbor, Michigan, around 1930. Its pointed grille, small flutes, and spoilers are designed to help branches flow around the machine. The entire machine (except for the hood and dash plate) is made of iron. Weight is an asset for tractors.

Even the tractors in this collection are streamlined. Tractors with this type of bodywork were designed for orchard use. This is a 1951 Massey Harris Model 44 Orchard tractor.

Think traction. But compared to a standard farm tractor, the Kaywood's dimensions are on the small side, just perfect for navigating the narrow rows between orchard trees. This particular unit features a Hercules six-cylinder engine hooked to Dodge Truck transmission parts. Chuck says, "This is an orphan, meaning that it's an off-brand that just about everybody has forgotten about. I haven't decided whether to restore it or not. I like people to see what tractors look like when you find them, and they don't look anything like my restored tractors, that's for sure."

Representing his collection of more than 90 tractors are three units restored to the tractor lover's equivalent of concours condition. The ultimate in streamlined tractors is Schneider's 1951 Massey Harris Model 44 Orchard tractor. There were approximately 124 built, and about 20 are known to still exist. As Chuck explains, "Everything was designed to deflect branches around the tractors and the operator. What makes restoring these so hard is that farmers often removed the fairings when they were damaged or rotted out. You never find tractors like these in complete condition, so these big pieces [referring to the fairing-like fenders] have to be fabricated from photographs and drawings."

Toy cars and trucks are parked on shelf after shelf. Each toy features the streamlined styling that Schneider favors. Nearly every toy is in original condition, whether it is nearly new or heavily enjoyed.

These two tractors were produced just before World War II by the Minneapolis-Moline Company. As described by Schneider, these are the Duesenbergs of tractors. Very few of either model are known to exist. Behind these distinctive tractors are spectacular signs. In the far background is a 30-foot sign rescued from a Detroit landmark, Bill's Donut Shop.

While not made for orchard duty like so many of the Schneiders' tractors, his two examples from Minneapolis-Moline are clearly anomalies. One of the company's concepts was to build a combination tractor and car. The thought was that a farmer could plow his fields during the week, then hose down the tractor on Saturday, and drive with the wife into town. Their concept debuted in 1938 and was known as the U Model Deluxe. The tractors were fully equipped for the road, with bumpers, headlights, turn signals, a horn, and everything else an automobile required to be licensed. The heated cab featured roll-down windows, a radio, and a jump seat. With a two-speed transfer case, the U Model Deluxe could hit 40 mph on the road.

The company produced approximately 100 of these unique creations, but at $3,800, the tractor cost more than a car and a tractor. Practical farmers stayed away in droves. For those who did test the concept, they found the cab to be extremely hot and noisy, as neither air conditioning nor insulation were part of the U Model design. Most U Model Deluxe tractors were returned to the factory, where their cabs were removed and discarded. The modified units were then returned to dealers as U Open models. Of the original 100 produced, only 20 or so are known to exist.

Even rarer than the U Model Deluxe is an original U Open Model. Schneider has one of each. Nearly identical to the cabbed version, the Open Model was thought to be sportier. Only 25 were produced. Only six are thought to remain.

Wearing the tired but happy look of a couple who has just finished a major creative project, Chuck says, "I really like putting things in some kind of setting, so they make sense. I'm not really into the sterile display where everything is just parked next to each other like a parking garage." Check and Diane have an affinity for saving and rescuing things they take a fancy to.

This travel trailer was custom built about 1932 for a wealthy Canadian business owner. The Schneiders found the trailer in near original condition and have used the posh creation for cross country trips.

Chuck tells the story of how he acquired their largest sign, measuring 30 feet, "Some days I'd take this route to work and I'd pass by Bill's Donut Shop that was on the corner of Woodward Avenue and Six Mile. It was a great place in its day, and they had this huge sign in front. One day, there's a crew there with a wrecking ball. I thought that it would be a shame to destroy that sign, so I stop my Ford and get out. I'm there in my suit and Gucci loafers, trying to find somebody in charge. I finally find the foreman and ask him, 'What would it take for you not to destroy the sign?' He was good with two hundred bucks. Later that day I had a friend stop by with a trailer to haul the sign away." Restored to its former glory, the sign occupies a long span of the Barn's north wall and is another artifact the couple have saved that represents the Detroit they know and still love.

The Schneiders have amassed an impressive collection of original (no reproduction) signs, mostly neon. The glow from their charged tubes casts great light over the collection of cars, trucks, tractors, and one travel trailer.

Their retro RV features a walnut parquet floor, a coffered barrel vaulted ceiling made of gum wood, built-in china cabinets, stained glass window decorations, and a coal-fired stove for heat. The trailer was custom built for a successful Canadian dairyman. He willed the trailer to his chauffeur, who may have appreciated the gesture but quickly sold the unit to the third owners. Around 1973, these owners built a garage around the trailer, effectively enshrining it. Chuck and Diane loosed the trailer soon after purchasing and making it roadworthy in 2001. In 2006, Diane participated in a cross-country road rally, rolling up thousands of miles with other antique trailer enthusiasts.

The Schneiders have assembled a genuinely fun collection of beautiful items that they enjoy sharing. Diane speaks for the couple when she says, "We like to enjoy these things. We take them out, use them, show them, and then have them here to enjoy with our friends. The best part of our lives is sharing this stuff. I mean, what's the good of having all of it if you don't share it?" ◆

Chapter 4
THE MOPAR CATHEDRAL

GARAGE OWNER: **JIM HOLDEN**

Some would call it coincidence, others providence. Standing in the driveway of Jim Holden's dream garage in Auburn Hills, Michigan, the headquarters of the company he once ran rises in the distance. "I remember looking out my office window on the top floor of that building and thinking about how great it would be to own this place," Holden says. His thoughts became reality, and it is undoubtedly great to be Jim Holden in the here and now.

Holden spent twenty years at Chrysler, working his way up through sales and marketing to the hallowed halls of the executive floor. In his last role at the corporation, he helped guide the automaker in his role as president and CEO of DaimlerChrysler in the turbulent period shortly after Daimler-Benz "merged" with the Chrysler Corporation.

However difficult that role was, Holden is relaxed these days, especially when he is in his inimitable garage with his stable of high-performance Mopars. "I first learned of the building when Lou Patane bought the place and began the conversion of the space," Holden remembers. Patane was hired into a marketing position at Chrysler in the early 1990s. He subsequently revitalized Mopar Performance and the company's racing program, including Dodge's return to NASCAR. Patane purchased the building in the late 1990s and did most of the physical conversion. Holden explains, "This was a Baptist church. It was built in 1965, at some point it was abandoned by its congregation. There used to be stained-glass windows where the cinder block is and pews bolted to the floor."

The soaring wood beams that support a load-bearing wood ceiling are still clearly visible. Patane added the garage doors that open high enough to accommodate a

The 1970 Plymouth AAR 'Cuda is exceptionally rare, being powered by a 340-cubic-inch V-8 topped with three two-barrel carburetors. This specific model was used to homologate Plymouth's race cars that competed in the original Sports Car Club of America Trans-Am Series.

Previous spread: Holden's collection contains a variety of Mopar muscle cars. While he favors E-Body Chryslers (Plymouth Barracudas and Dodge Challengers), he also has a 1971 Dodge Charger and a 2003 Dodge Viper.

complete semi tractor with a 53-foot trailer. When Patane moved on to another job outside of Chrysler, Holden purchased the building. The year was 1998.

Because the space was already converted for garage use, Holden did nothing but move in a vehicle lift and additional tools to help him with his ongoing projects. He also added lots of lights, which do an excellent job of transforming the space from a practical garage to a welcoming display/party area. As for how he uses the space, Holden says, "The standing joke is that my wife puts both the dog and me out at 7 a.m. and lets us back in at 6 p.m., so I've gotta have someplace to go and something to do. This is it." He continues, "Now that I'm retired, I'd go crazy if I didn't have something to tear apart, so I come here."

His project cars are quite remarkable, and reflect his time spent at Chrysler as well as his mechanical handy work. "I spent a lot of time with engineers, so even though I'm not an engineer, I'm a pretty good backyard engineer," Holden modestly states. Proof of his engineering acumen is easily found in his son's 1971 Dodge Charger R/T.

Holden purchased the car from one of his compatriots at Chrysler. Holden says, "I got it from a tech guy at Viper Tech Center. It was a good original car with 440 Magnum [7.2 liters and a four-barrel carburetor], 4.10:1 gears, steel wheels, and bottle-caps [hubcaps]. It sat a lot, so every time you nailed it, something else fell off." Given the car's advanced age (it was purchased in 1998), its condition was to be expected. Holden and his son went

through the entire car, rebuilding the engine, bringing all of the vital systems up to perfect working condition, and sprucing up the exterior.

Literally days after the renovation was complete, Holden's son was driving through a congested construction area and a gravel hauler smashed into the Charger. Holden's son was unhurt, but the Charger was totaled by the insurance company. With a portion of his insurance check, Holden purchased the Charger back from the insurer and brought it back to life again. "The second time through, we got the car looking even better than when we did it the first time," Holden points out. He and his son also did some other mechanical upgrades, including the fitment of rear disc brakes and a Keisler five-speed manual

Looking better than when it came out of the factory in 1971, this Dodge Charger R/T is owned by Holden's son. If cars were cats, this one only has seven lives left. The Holdens originally saved it from a slow death of normal decomposition, and resurrected it a second time after a dump truck totaled it.

transmission in place of the original TorqueFlite three-speed automatic. "I don't know how we ever used to drive these cars on the highway with their short gears," Holden comments, a bit bemused. "The overdrive on the new Keisler makes all the difference, and makes this a really good highway car, even with the 4.10 gear."

Another piece of clever engineering is Holden's 1970 Challenger convertible. This Dodge, painted Plum Crazy purple, has a V-10 engine where a diminutive V-8 used to reside. The conversion had already been completed before he purchased the car at a Barrett-Jackson auction. Partly. "I think the guy who did the engine swap was on a tight deadline to get the car ready for the auction, so while the major engineering was well done, almost nothing else was," Holden explains.

After countless hours of ingenious problem solving and engineering, the Challenger now has brakes and instruments that work. Holden points out, "The car came

Memories and memorabilia from Holden's 30-year career at Ford, Chrysler, and DaimlerChrysler are displayed around his garage space. The Viper is a 2003 that Holden uses as his primary transportation in the summer.

When the banks of fluorescent lights are on, the garage takes on a utilitarian flavor. The original church's architecture can be seen clearly in the structure's wooden, load-bearing ceiling. One can imagine the stained glass that used to fill the space between the vertical wood columns.

Holden is at home in his converted church. When he is not working on his Mopars, this ex-president of DaimlerChrysler finds time to serve on multiple boards and help launch startup commercial ventures.

with many parts salvaged from the wrecked 1997 Viper GTS donor car, including the gauges. I took them and integrated them into the Challenger's original dash, but wired it to make them backlit—Challengers didn't originally have backlit gauges." Tapping into his network at DaimlerChrysler, Holden completely retrofitted the rest of the interior, using modified seats from a Dodge Neon SRT-4 and having them covered in leather-like vinyl to give the interior a proper circa-1970 feel. Holden also points out the custom-installed audio receiver that features Sirius Satellite Radio—Holden sits on that company's board.

Holden seems to methodically complete one system at a time, and he points out how he'll spend the next season, "My next challenge is the A/C. The car is an original A/C car, but it's going to take some work to hook it all up." Holden explains what makes the effort worth it, "When you first drive up to a cruise or a show, people think 'Gee, there's a nice old Challenger convertible' and then they notice all of the things that are different on this car, the seats, gauges, and then you open the hood and that always draws a crowd."

Holden's 1970 Challenger began life with a 318-cubic-inch V-8 under the hood. That space is now occupied by a 488-cubic-inch V-10 transplanted from a 1997 Dodge Viper. A six-speed manual gearbox backs up the motor.

Holden's variety of E-Body cars shows why these cars have remained popular for decades. Slight variations give each model a distinct look. Every model is 1970, with the AAR 'Cuda at the front, followed by the Viper-powered Challenger Convertible and a Challenger Coupe.

Built in 1965 as a Baptist church, Jim Holden's garage is no longer a house of worship, but it does contain near sacred elements from bygone days of the original Chrysler Corporation. DaimlerChrysler's Auburn Hills headquarters can be seen in the distance.

While the Charger and Viper-powered Challenger have been major projects, the balance of Holden's collection is already in excellent shape. His 1970 Challenger coupe is a force to be reckoned with thanks to its 440 Six-Pack. This triple-carbureted big block produces 390 horsepower and was preferred by many to the mighty Mopar 426-cubic-inch Hemi because of the 440's superior drivability. The yellow 1970 AAR 'Cuda also generates impressive power from a Six-Pack–configured engine. From a displacement of only 340 cubic inches, the motor puts out 290 horsepower.

Holden's collection constantly changes, but when asked why he has what he does, his logic is clear. "What draws you to these is that they were what you wanted when you were a kid. Once I got through the 1970s, there really wasn't anything fun to drive, so these old cars were it. It was the performance thrill. As a kid, I just drooled for any kind of performance. Everything newer was anemic. These cars weren't, so that's what I have."

If you're ever in Detroit for the annual Woodward Dream Cruise, look for Holden. You'll probably spot him behind the wheel of one of these. Smiling. ◆

Chapter 5
FULL THROTTLE

GARAGE OWNER: **DON SOENEN**

When Don Soenen sets his sights on something, he goes after it at full throttle. No compromises accepted. After touring his garage in Plymouth, Michigan, about 45 minutes west of Detroit, it's obvious that his garage space is a manifestation of this approach toward life.

Driving onto Soenen's property, it is impossible to tell that the garage space was added to the original home. Even though his home was originally built with two attached garages that could accommodate as many as six vehicles, Soenen wanted a dedicated space to augment the enjoyment of his hobby.

Completed in 2005, the new space is generously sized to hold the six non-daily drivers Soenen keeps at home, plus a row of motorcycles. Designed as a place for parties or to kick back with other enthusiasts, the garage boasts a large flat-screen plasma monitor and surround-sound audio system. A fully functional custom-built 1950s-style soda bar decorated in a Coke motif helps keep guests satisfied with refreshments. Should musical tastes favor the oldies, a perfectly restored jukebox sits loaded with 45s that are ready to drop and spin.

Not content to decorate his garage in an expected manner, Soenen commissioned a startlingly realistic three-dimensional mural to cover one entire wall. The mural is one continuous image. Beginning at the front of his garage, the scene depicts an old Mobilgas service station. The characters painted into the scene include Soenen's own father, who is shown standing in the open doorway. Moving toward the rear of the building, a Chevrolet Bel Air and Corvette are being worked on in the service bays. The scene continues, and where the faux Mobil station ends, an open field is painted, with Soenen's boyhood home depicted in the background.

The mural causes any number of double takes due to the skill with which it was completed and because Soenen has strategically placed period correct elements on the face of the mural. A Mobilgas Pegasus outlined with red neon draws your attention, as does the hanging Greyhound Lines sign. An antique Coke machine sits out front ready to quench your thirst in exchange for a dime. An operational air pump and a pristine 6-volt battery charger look ready to service customers. The illusion is powerful.

In contrast, Soenen's cars are anything but illusions. His Superformance Cobra and Plymouth Prowler are what he calls his "fun" cars. Soenen is straightforward about his Cobra, "This is one of the best values on the market. For the price, I don't know where else you can get this kind of performance and attention." Soenen had his delivered as a rolling chassis and promptly dropped a 351-cubic-inch Ford Windsor V-8 in the engine bay. He estimates that with the modifications he's made to the engine (it now displaces 390 cubes), it could be producing as much as 600 horsepower.

Regarding the Prowler, Soenen says, "When it came out, it just caught my eye. I had to have one. They're just a lot of fun. It's not big power, but because of the way it's geared, it's really quick out of the hole. The trailer is a pretty cool accessory, too."

Since they were announced by Ford Motor Company, Soenen also wanted a new Ford GT and Shelby GT500

Above: Soenen commissioned a mural to be painted on one entire wall of the garage. The pictured section shows two open service bays of the imaginary Mobilgas service station. Antique equipment placed "outside" the painted image help complete the carefully crafted illusion.

Previous spread: Located West of Detroit, Don Soenen's garage blends old and new in a comfortable space for cars, motorcycles, and people.

Mustang. His opportunity to acquire them came in the summer of 2006. Busy working for a local charity, Soenen was soliciting donations from his town's Lincoln-Mercury dealer. As the conversation turned to cars, Soenen let it be known that he was looking to purchase a GT, Ford's 200-mph supercar. While he wanted one, he let the dealer know that he wouldn't pay over sticker, and that he'd also like to purchase a limited-edition Shelby GT500 along with the GT. It just so happens that the brother of the Lincoln-Mercury dealer owns the local Ford dealership, and a phone call was made. Soon after, both new cars were in Soenen's hands. He raves about their performance, quality, and styling.

Unlike some owners of ultra-high performance cars, Soenen has proven himself capable of handling them. Shelves of racing trophies, medallions, and a beautiful

Don Soenen leans back in the doorway of his own Mobilgas service station. Soenen's father is pictured in the doorway, while Soenen's uncle tends the cash register.

Rolex watch attest to Soenen's skill behind the wheel. Soenen opens up about his start in racing, "Back in 1998, I knew I wanted to go racing, so I attended eight different driving schools that year. I made the rounds and did them all, from the Bob Bondurant school to Skip Barber and Panoz." At one of those schools, Soenen met a fellow student who was racing retired stock cars in so-called vintage

racing events. It would take less than a year for Soenen to purchase his first race car, enter his first race, experience his first crash, purchase three more race cars, and form his own racing team.

The terms "vintage" and "historic" are used loosely in the type of racing Soenen does. It is enough to understand that the series is populated by non-current but fully

Anchored by his vintage stock cars, Don Soenen's garage clearly demonstrates the way this racer approaches life. The cars are parked on a custom tiled floor, and a three-dimensional mural runs the length of one wall.

Betty Boop waits on patrons of Soenen's soda fountain. Visitors enjoy tunes from the restored jukebox and the many original paintings done by Scott Jacobs.

This Cobra is classified as a kit car. Produced by Superformance, the complete, painted rolling chassis was delivered without a drivetrain. Soenen's race shop installed a powerful Ford V-8 estimated to produce 600 horsepower.

modern ex-professional race cars from various racing series, including NASCAR, Busch, and the Sports Car Club of America (SCCA). Soenen's first race car was a Ford Taurus stock car once campaigned by Brett Bodine. Soon after he bought it, when preparing for his first race at the challenging Moroso Motorsports Park in Florida, Soenen stuffed the Taurus into the wall at the end of the front straight. Soenen recalls, "It was my first practice session, and I had been turning some pretty good times. But then I went into turn number one way too fast and locked up the brakes. I skidded right off the end of the track, hit

hard, and wrecked the car pretty badly. The corner worker told me that in eleven years of spotting races at that corner, he had never seen anybody hit the wall that hard."

Explaining that he didn't want to miss the next race of the series that he had just entered, Soenen purchased another ex-race car, this one a Chevrolet Lumina once campaigned by Ricky Craven. The balance of Soenen's first season went much better. It wouldn't take long for Soenen Motorsports to win its first race. For several years, Soenen campaigned more than one car, with others piloted by professional "hot shoes" and fellow gentlemen racers.

When the Plymouth Prowler debuted in 1997, Soenen liked the styling so much that he had to have one. He loves the fact that it is a practical hot rod.

Soenen's stock cars include an ex–Brett Bodine Ford Taurus (foreground) and an ex–Ricky Craven Chevrolet Lumina. The awards and photos on the back wall document Soenen's many on-track victories and podium finishes since he began racing in 1999.

The newest additions to Soenen's collection include a 2006 Ford GT and 2007 Shelby GT500 Mustang. Together, the cars boast 1,050 horsepower. The GT wins honors for being the fastest car in the garage with a certified top speed of more than 200 mph.

Soenen's garage even looks good at night. An original Standard Oil of New York sign is positioned above a vintage Standard gas pump in a vignette that looks like a country gas station.

Today, Soenen is a respected member in the historic/vintage racing community.

Both of Soenen's stock cars are on display in his garage and are still in ready-to-race condition. Along with the stockers, Soenen also purchased road racing cars that once competed in the SCCA Trans Am series. Soenen explains, "My Trans Am cars make about the same power as the stock cars, but they weigh considerably less, so they're a lot faster." Soenen regularly races these cars, and they are kept at a race shop in the nearby city of Livonia.

Soenen continues to work on his driving skills, and is still a frequent student at racing schools around the country. Soenen notes, "Fortunately, my companies and the great people who run them afford me the opportunity to pursue my dreams." Soenen owns two multinational manufacturing companies that produce meteorological and emissions instrumentation. Soenen's behavior reveals much about his approach to life, especially considering that Soenen won the coveted Rolex Endurance Series Historic Championship in 2006. One might think that he didn't need any more training. Soenen proudly displays the superlative chronometer that comes with the Rolex Championship. It shares space with dozens of other racing trophies and framed images of his cars at speed on tracks across the country.

While the garage is complete, Soenen is apt to change anything at anytime should something better or more interesting come along. If he takes an interest in another facet of the automotive world, the garage could change dramatically and quickly. Such is the life of one who operates at full throttle, full time. ◆

Chapter 6
THE AUTO SPA

GARAGE OWNER: **SHAMEL RUSHWIN**

Detroit provided opportunity for generations of hard-working people. Shamel Rushwin is one who made the most of the opportunities Detroit served up. Born into the family of a Lebanese immigrant father, Shamel had his first encounter with Detroit in 1966 at the then-new General Motors assembly plant in Lordstown, Ohio, where he worked on the line. GM builds Chevrolet Cobalts there today, but Rushwin has long since moved on from his initial position, tenaciously improving his skills and putting them to use for Volkswagen, DaimlerChrysler, and finally Ford Motor Company.

Rushwin begins his story by saying, "I have always been crazy about cars. When I was a young kid, my passion was building 1/18th- and 1/27th-scale model cars, making them as perfect as you possibly could." He continues, "Building those models was almost prophetic, as I would work my way up from an assembly line job to being a corporate vice president at both DaimlerChrysler and Ford, and one day be ultimately responsible for the assembly of 45,000 vehicles a day all over the world—Europe, Asia Pacific, South America, and here in North America. It's a realization of a dream, from building those little model cars by hand, to building real cars on that kind of scale."

Rushwin's senior positions at DaimlerChrysler and Ford required much from this senior-level manager. In turn, these companies compensated him with the means to acquire a number of the world's most desirable supercars. "When I was still at DaimlerChrysler, my wife and I decided to build our dream house. She got things like walk-in his and hers closets and a gourmet kitchen. I got a garage." Rushwin happily recounts the process, "Just as important as having space for at least six bays was being

Above: The content of the spa makes it clear that Rushwin favors modern supercars. An electric four-post lift makes detailing and servicing the cars easier, and provides room for the storage of a fourth car.

Previous spread: Set atop a hill within an exclusive gated subdivision, Shamel Rushwin's home includes two separate garages that share a motor court. Rushwin's automotive spa occupies the space farthest to the right. His everyday cars are parked in the three bays to the left.

able to enjoy the area as living space. I really think of this as an automotive spa." As he defines the characteristics of his spa, he ticks off the residence-style heating and cooling systems, the four-post electric lift, the complete set of tools, and air compressor. "There's really very little I can't do in here maintenance wise," Rushwin notes.

While utility is important, Rushwin explains the totality of what he created, "The space really represents me—my DNA and my 38 years in the automotive business—I like being in here as much, if not more than, any other place in

The garage's floor space easily accommodates three vehicles with ample room surrounding them. Windows flood the space with natural light, giving the space an open, airy feel.

Rushwin keeps his vehicles in perfect condition. While his Ferrari 550 Maranello looks as though it's never been on the road, the car has accumulated several thousand miles, several hundred of which were accrued at high-speed Ferrari Club track events.

The wheel of a Ferrari 550 Maranello provides a dramatic backdrop that set off the red valve covers of Rushwin's 1995 Dodge Viper. Illustrating Rushwin's passion for speed, the Viper's V-10 features multiple upgrades from John Hennessy, and churns out approximately 550 horsepower.

my house." Features that contribute to the space's comfort include a flat-screen TV, a stereo, and a refrigerator. Built-in cabinets store a small library of books, a collection of automotive magazines, and items such as fitted luggage for his Ferrari and a fireproof Nomex racing suit. Rushwin's competition driver's license from the Sports Car Club of America (SCCA) hangs on a wall inside the garage, along with pictures of him competing in races and driving his personal cars at private track days hosted by the Ferrari Club.

As Rushwin walks through his garage, it becomes clear he has a true affinity for iconic supercars. Beginning with his 1995 Viper, he explains why he has each car, "I had a lot to do with the car's manufacturing, and it gives me a lot of pride, as it has a part of me in it. I'll keep this car forever because it's a modern classic." Revealing his intimate knowledge of cars and manufacturing, he readily admits to the Viper's relatively crude engineering, lack of refined features (it has no side windows, but uses old-fashioned snap-in plastic side curtains), and brutish power. "I really love to cruise Woodward Avenue in it. Everybody wants to race you." Detroit's Woodward Avenue is one of the best-known roads in American automotive lore, and it remains the site of one of the world's largest automotive events in the world today, the Woodward Dream Cruise.

Rushwin's Ferrari 550 Maranello provides a dramatic contrast to the Viper. The latter is rude, crude, and misbehaved in comparison to the former's high level of design. While the Viper out muscles the Maranello, the aerodynamic

Rushwin owns a 2005 Ford GT for the same reason he owns the Viper—he had a hand in bringing both cars to market. At Ford and DaimlerChrysler, Rushwin helped develop innovative low-volume manufacturing processes that played a significant role in making these cars a reality.

Once used as a prop in the famous "Little Rascals" series of film shorts that first aired in 1922, this Steelcraft pedal car was purchased from Dick Kughn's collection and was subsequently restored to its perfected condition.

refinement and sophisticated engineering give the Ferrari a much higher top speed. This leather-lined missile represents only the latest in a long line of Italian exotics that Rushwin has owned. When Chrysler owned Lamborghini, Rushwin made the most of his corporate position and owned a 1988 1/2 Countach and later a 1992 Diablo. Among former Ferrari models, he also owned one of the 273 GTOs produced between 1984 and 1987. Rushwin recalls, "That car was just so perfect. It wasn't legal to drive on the road in the United States, but I drove it at track days and around our gated community. You know, the cops can't come in here, so we had some fun with it." After driving around Rushwin's neighborhood, we doubt he ever approached the 288's top speed of 190 mph during his short outings.

The yellow 2005 Ford GT is Rushwin's latest acquisition. Like the Viper, he had a hand in the car's production. Referencing the color, he explains, "I liked the yellow because it's a low runner, and because it was just like the first GT they showed at the Detroit Auto Show in 2002."

In addition to the full-size cars in the garage, Rushwin is just as proud of his tike-sized pedal cars. A beautifully detailed Lincoln Phaeton sports a six-wheel design (it has two spare tires), dual mirrors, spotlights, horns, and

This elegant Lincoln Dual Cowl Phaeton was once just a child's toy. Rushwin restored it to better than original condition, and remains amazed at the detail executed by the Steelcraft company.

Looking over the 550-horsepower supercharged V-8 of the Ford GT, built-in cabinetry holds a variety of items, including photos, a collection of magazines, and fitted luggage for the 550 Maranello.

whitewall tires. Clearly his favorite is a little two-tone roadster. Manufactured by the Steelcraft Company, Rushwin produces a yellowed clipping from a movie trade industry paper. The page shows the cast of the famous Little Rascals surrounding his car.

Rushwin purchased the car from noted Detroit collector Dick Kughn (featured in Chapter 14) in 2003. Explaining the purchase, he said, "I really wanted something from Kughn's Carail Collection because his place meant so much to the industry and to me."

After talking about the pedal cars, the conversation turns to how Rushwin involves his growing family in his life's passion. Three of his four children are sons. During the summer, Rushwin offers, "It's not unusual for me to get the boys in these cars and do a lap of Oakland County." The sight of these three cars on the open road must turn plenty of heads. He adds, "I also like to drive the cars on regular errands, like when I pick my granddaughter up from school. The looks I get from the kids standing in line is just too much."

Rushwin is clearly not stuck in the past, as he continually adds new photos of recent events and outings. With more than 1,500 horsepower available to him, there seems little chance that he'll slow down anytime soon. "Cars are my life. I don't know what I'd do without them," Rushwin concludes. Amen to that, brother. ◆

Chapter 7
THE HORSE TRADER

GARAGE OWNER: **GREG ORNAZIAN**

Photography by Bobby Alcott & Rex Roy

The disease started for me when I was 15. My godfather gave me his sister's 1959 Thunderbird. It was nothing more than a pile of rust, but I couldn't wait to drive, so I did a 'so-called' restoration on it with two of my friends. The day I turned 16, it was ready." Greg Ornazian's maiden voyage took place in 1971. His everyday ride has improved markedly since the oxidized T-Bird, and he has amassed a small collection of important American vehicles in the years since he humbly began.

Ornazian grew up in Maryland, but moved away after he realized that his degree in education would never put him in the wheels he sought. Family and the love of cars brought him to Detroit in 1978, when he landed a sales job working for a successful tool and die company. Years later, Ornazian is still selling, but now he does it for the tool and die company he owns.

Selling came naturally. Ornazian tells the story of how his first successful flip began. "When I was a teen, I worked four jobs at once. One of them was at a gas station, so I learned about cars hands-on back then. One of my other jobs was mowing lawns. Between them all, I saved a pretty good chunk of change that I used to buy my first car sight unseen. Can you believe it?" He smiles at the memory, "I was so naïve. My favorite car of all time was a 1967 Corvette, and I thought that since a '68 was just a year newer, the cars would be almost identical."

For those unfamiliar with Corvette history, 1967 was the last year of the second-generation Corvette and 1968 was the year Chevrolet introduced the all-new third-generation model. The cars were nothing alike. Ornazian continues, "I went to look at the car, and while its owner had to explain to me why the 1968 didn't look like a 1967, I bought the car

Nestled off a main suburban artery sits the home Greg Ornazian designed and built in 1996. Attached to the right of the main house sits a 60-foot-wide garage that is a full 33 feet deep. It currently houses 12 cars and several motorcycles.

Previous spread: Greg Ornazian's garage houses a collection of high-performance automobiles spanning nearly 80 years.

anyway. It took a lot of lawns to equal the $2,400 I paid for that car." Just months later, Ornazian flipped the Corvette for a tidy $800 profit. Thus began Ornazian's first career move into sales. "Buying and selling cars put me through college," he says. He estimates that since the 1970s he's bought and sold about 150 vehicles, mostly Corvettes and Volkswagen Beetles.

"I'd get a Corvette when I wanted to go fast, and then I'd get tired of being poor from getting tickets and burning lots of gas. So then I'd buy a Bug," Ornazian explains. "I could make money on either because there were always people who wanted to buy those cars." The types of vehicles Ornazian deals with today are a bit more exotic than his early flips. Corvettes remain a favorite, as one can see by looking at his current collection housed within his home's attached 33-foot-deep by 60-foot-wide garage.

One of the first cars to catch your eye is a striking blue 1964 Corvette convertible. Its condition is certified

Bloomington Gold, the recognized standard for Corvettes. While in exceptional condition, the distinguishing characteristic is its Z06 option package. It was the only Corvette convertible built with that option in 1964, making it a one-of-one example. The headline feature for the Z06 option package is the fuel-injected 327-cubic-inch V-8—a small block that delivered the horsepower punch of a big block.

Other rare Corvettes share space with the 1963, including three with racing history. The oldest is a 1961 that campaigned in the livery of Gulf Gasoline throughout the early 1960s. Pilots of this racer included the famous Don Yenko and Dr. Dick Thompson. The car's number 11 represents its trips to victory lane, including a significant win at Sebring, Florida. Recognizing the car's important place in Corvette history, it has already been inducted into the Bloomington Gold Corvette Hall of Fame.

Ornazian's next racing Corvette is the 1968 BF Goodrich Lifesaver Radial #49. While equipped with a powerful L88-code 427-cubic-inch big block V-8, this car never turned a lap in anger. The car was supposedly used for press and promotional purposes, but Ornazian

Three double doors provide access to Ornazian's collection. Since he drives his vehicles on a regular basis, the access is necessary. The 1955 Chevrolet Nomad in the foreground is a rare exterior color, Navaho Tan.

Ornazian's collection favors two-seat coupes and convertibles. Examples run the gamut from a classic supercharged 1937 Cord 812 Phaeton to a 2005 Lamborghini Murcielago Roadster.

An award-winning 1935 Auburn Boattail Speedster shares garage space with two of Ornazian's motorcycles: a stock 1994 Harley-Davidson Nostalgia Fat Boy and a heavily customized 2003 Harley-Davidson 100th Anniversary Night Train.

cautions that tracking the originality of race cars is a tricky business, "Experts have looked at this car, and we think that that is what this car must have been because of details like its ultra rare BF Goodrich racing tires." This Corvette's sister vehicles were campaigned by John Greenwood Racing, a team that specialized in racing Corvettes across the globe. In its day, a racer prepped like Ornazian's was clocked at more than 170 mph in the famed French endurance classic, the 24 Hours of Le Mans.

Ornazian's newest racing Corvette sports an extensive competition logbook. In 1987, Corvettes were so successful on racetracks that the Sports Car Club of America (SCCA) banned them from general competition for 1988 and 1989. Not to be put off, Corvette racers started their own one-make series known as the Corvette Challenge. Chevrolet participated in the series by building special cars for racers in 1988 and 1989. Of the 60 identical units built in 1989 with the factory racing option R7F, Ornazian's Corvette was one of only 29 cars transformed into a competition car. Four-time Sport Car Champion Andy Pilgrim drove Ornazian's car in 1989, and tallied

Decked out in full racing regalia, this 1968 Corvette L88 promotes BF Goodrich Lifesaver Radials. This was one of just a handful built, but it never turned a wheel in competition because of its advertising duties.

a win at Road Atlanta and several other high-ranking finishes. "I really wanted one of the Corvette Challenge Cars, and this one's Detroit heritage made it perfect for me," Ornazian states. The #18 Corvette proudly wears the logos of Stroh's Beer (once a major Detroit brewery) and Mr. B's Pub (a Detroit eatery favored by racers). The Corvette still sees occasional track duty, as Ornazian has a vintage racing license.

While he likes going fast, Ornazian also knows how to appreciate going slowly. His cruisers include a perfect 1956 Ford Thunderbird that recently emerged from a five-year, every-nut-and-bolt restoration. His 1955 Chevrolet Nomad came from the family of the original owner. The massive 1960 Cadillac convertible makes the perfect

Ornazian's love for art deco styling put this perfect 1937 Cord 812 Phaeton in his garage. Details include the coffin-shaped nose and the hidden headlamps that are opened via a crank from the cockpit.

This 1969 Corvette is one of Ornazian's favorite drivers. With the 435-horsepower code L88 427-cubic-inch big block, power is not an issue. Ornazian modified several details to make the car more comfortable, including adding radial tires and opening up the exhaust.

Memorabilia, posters, and photos occupy spaces where cars aren't. The Union 76 pump looks ready to supply racing fuel to the fuel-injected engine of Ornazian's 1961 Corvette race car.

parade car. As he looks over his collection he muses, "I really need one more car to make this collection complete. I have almost all of the two-seat American sports cars that I want, except I'm missing a Duesenberg to go with my Cord and my Auburn. The problem is that Duesenbergs are million-dollar cars these days." While the tool and die business is good, these days it's not *that* good.

Ornazian's two striking art deco classics are a 1935 Auburn Boattail Speedster and a 1937 Cord 812 Phaeton. American designer Gordon Buehrig penned both shapes. Like Duesenbergs, the Auburn and Cord were built in Indiana. Both are rolling masterpieces of American style and engineering. These cars contrast dramatically with two of Ornazian's outliers, a 1968 Volkswagen Beetle and a 2005 Lamborghini Murcielago. Ornazian explains, "I have the Bug because it reminds me of the cars I used to have. This one is cool because the exterior is styled like a 1953 model. The Lambo is something my youngest son turned me on to, and this roadster is exactly what I would have

Ornazian's collection spills out of his garage into his recreation room. Against the backdrop of banners and posters, a small but formidable collection of early motorcycles rest on their kick stands.

Of all of his cars, these vintage pedal cruisers get the least use—Ornazian is too big to fit in them. Their restorations may not have been as complex as some of his full-size cars, but these examples show the same attention to detail that characterize every one of Ornazian's vehicles.

Greg Ornazian casually leans against his Bloomington Gold Certified 1964 Corvette. "I drive it—so I'm not going to lean against it?" The 1970 American Motors AMX in the background is another love from his teenage years.

ordered if I had bought it new." The 2005 Italian exotic boasts a 580-horsepower V-12 and a six-speed manual. Ornazian purchased it at an auction, and uses it often when the weather is clear and warm.

Ornazian worked hard to find the cars he has, and he is sincerely comfortable with them. "I do show them, but they're not trailer queens. If I can get to a show within about two hours, I'll drive cars there. It's what they were built for." With his experience at trading, buying, and selling, his collection may look very different as the years progress, but it will certainly not become any less interesting. ◆

Chapter 8
AN ARTIST'S SPACE

GARAGE OWNER: **BUCK MOOK**

While striding into his mid-60s, Buck Mook readily admits, "I'm still living like I'm in high school." Just as carefree kids decorate their rooms and school lockers, Mook's entire home clearly exhibits the passion of his life. Even his cats reflect his focus, named after milestone Studebakers—Champion, Hawk, Lark, and Commander.

Well-liked by all in Detroit's car community, the soft-spoken designer knew what he wanted to do when he was just a kid. Mook reflects, "I always wanted to be either a car designer or an architect. But growing up back in New Jersey where everything is Revolutionary Era, it's kind of hard to be an architect who likes to build new stuff, so it seemed like cars would be my thing. So, I went after it and did my dream." Before he was 10, the puzzle pieces that would lead him to Detroit started falling together. He explains, "There was a Ford plant in the town where I grew up, and my parents always knew the plant manager, so I got tours all the time. This was one of the things that made me want to work for Ford. I hired in right after I graduated from the Art Center College of Design in California in 1967. I retired thirty years later."

Mook's home is situated on a picturesque inland lake north of Detroit. One look at the place reveals the fact that Mook is a designer and an artist. Open any of the garage doors and vivid colors blast off the canvases that cover almost every inch of wall space. Where the average garage might have a familiar Mobil Oil Pegasus, Mook hangs his original art. The effect is stunning, and one could easily overlook Mook's cars for the engaging art.

The garage looks like a new structure, and Mook tells a familiar tale common to car collectors. It includes stories of

Buck Mook's main garage holds nine cars, including his 1949 Cadillac Series 62 convertible. Mook's own artwork dominates the space, adding color and an energy to the surroundings.

Previous spread: Buck Mook's daily vehicle sits in the drive, seemingly admiring his collection of art and cars.

various storage facilities and not being able to keep beloved four-wheeled possessions within easy reach. Mook decided to consolidate. "I originally bought the house because it had a double-decker garage." The home site—once a cottage and a general store for the one-time vacation community before that—is built on a hill. The two-story main garage is actually built into the hill, with lower and upper levels facing opposite sides of the hill to make use of the incline.

Mook continues, "But since I have around 24 cars, I really needed more spaces in one place—my cars were stored everywhere. I decided to build the new attached garage back in 2004, and started making drawings and models. I wrapped the garage around the existing house, and now I have way more square footage of garage area than I do inside the house."

The cars in Mook's collection reflect the same variety seen in his art. There's a little bit of everything. Mook

explains, "I wanted to have a car from every decade, so that's what I've done. But right now I'm missing something from the 1930s." One gets the impression that the open slot will soon be filled.

Mook's oldest car is his 1903 Michigan. Originally produced in Kalamazoo, the Michigan was one of only 150 made. Only three are known to survive today. Mook traced his car back to its first owner, and he learned that the famous automobile collector William Harrah of Nevada gaming fame also once owned the car. Of the many awards won by the little car, it most recently took a Lion's trophy at the Meadow Brook Concours d'Elegance.

The second oldest car in Mook's garage is the somewhat imposing 1907 Stoddard-Dayton. With a massive 4.6-liter four-cylinder engine, this car was all about speed. Based on extensive research, Mook believes his car won the 1907 Glidden Tour endurance

Mook's goal is to have a car from every decade. While he is currently missing something from the 1930s, his 1927 and 1928 Marmon race cars from Uruguay do an admirable job of representing the Roaring Twenties—especially when they fire up.

Parked by the nose of his Cadillac, Mook's 1903 Michigan looks even tinier than it is. The car, in original condition, is one of only three known to exist. It was once owned by the famous collector William Harrah.

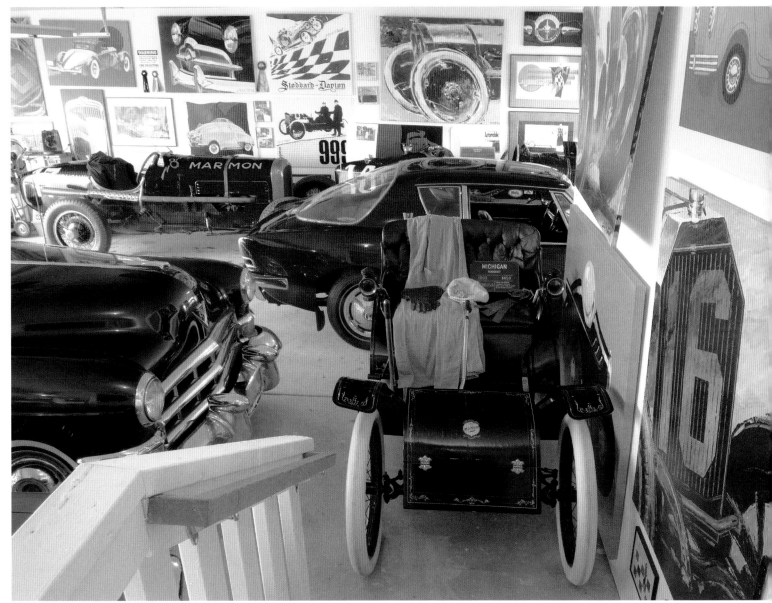

Purchased new because he liked its style, Mook never really enjoyed driving his steel-bodied 1977 Ferrari 308 GTB. He vastly prefers piloting his 1907 Stoddard-Dayton race car, one of only two known to exist.

race, the most significant automotive event of the day. The only other known model identical to Mook's is on display at Chicago's Science and Industry Museum.

Representing the Roaring Twenties are a pair of truly unusual cars: racing Marmons. As Mook tells the story, the cars (originally sedans) were exported to a Marmon dealer in Uruguay. To attract attention for his franchise, the dealer converted the cars to compete in local Grand Prix–style races. Sometime in the 1990s, an American collector repatriated the cars, and then Mook acquired them. Mook exercises the cars every summer, much to the delight of the children in his neighborhood. The exhaust from the mighty straight eight-cylinder engines sounds like nothing else on the road.

Recognizing its status as a design icon, Mook owns a 1949 Cadillac Series 62 convertible. A strong argument can be made that this car, with its kicked-up taillights, started the fin fad in America that ran all through the 1950s.

Mook's vehicles representing the 1950s were off-site, but the 1960s were well represented with two interesting, if not particularly rare, cars. Purchased from an aging

Mook's collection currently stands at around two dozen cars and an additional two dozen boats. This Chris Craft runabout sees lake duty every summer when it is moored in front of Mook's home.

Living as a bachelor, Mook gets away with having this type of décor for his living room. A grille from a Mustang II, one of Mook's designs, is mounted above the fireplace.

All of Mook's rooms are decorated with car art, car parts, toy cars, and model cars. Valuable antique children's toys, including two 1934 Chrysler Airflows, are mounted on the wall above the museum-quality print of a Ferrari 308 similar to Mook's own GTB.

Working as a designer at Ford Motor Company for 30 years, Mook never had an office with a window. Today, his seat behind his drawing board looks out over one of the most beautiful lakes in the county.

Situated on an inland lake north of Detroit, Mook boasts that he has more garage space than living space. The structure to the right is a two-story garage, providing room for four vehicles.

widow who owned the car since it was new, Mook's 1964 Studebaker Avanti is completely original from its paint to its carpeting. The only things ever changed in the engine are the oil and radiator fluid. Mook notes, "This is one of only 58 made with the new grille that came out in 1964, but it still has the old-style round headlights. I'm guessing the headlight supplier for Studebaker was late on a delivery, so they built the first few that year with the old lamps."

Mook also enjoys his 1965 Thunderbird. He bought it for its beautifully designed interior. Mook recalls, "When I was working on designing Thunderbirds at Ford, we never had any money to do anything cool. But look inside this car—everything is cool; the way the interior wraps around, the way the instruments light up at night, and even the headliner is cool."

In addition to the 1973 Mustang awaiting restoration (plus a couple of station wagons that Mook actually admits to liking), representing the decade of the '70s is a 1977 Ferrari 308 GTB. Mook is a bit bemused as he explains, "I bought the car new because I just loved the way it looked. And I still do. But I just never really liked driving it." Showing very few miles, the neglected Ferrari looks a bit tired, as evidenced by its rubber bumper guards literally falling off due to nothing more than the force of gravity. Mook thinks it might be time to restore it, now that most people have forgotten about the TV show *Magnum P.I.*

Cars are clearly not relegated to Mook's garage. Walking in his home through any door, one sees nothing but models, die-cast car nameplates and emblems, and seemingly random car parts everywhere. Even the archways between rooms are lined with drawings, newspaper articles, magazine clippings, and photos of cars—Mook's cars, friends' cars, and those of other enthusiasts. The original drawing that got him hired into Ford in 1967 shares wall space with a 1912 oil painting from France depicting a woman at the wheel of an automobile, and original artwork used in car catalogs and advertisements up through the 1960s. There are also promotional photographs of the MonkeeMobile and the Green Hornet car, two famous Hollywood television series cars that Mook helped design while he was still in college.

Mook is a man who has lived, and continues to live, his dream. He looks as comfortable with this Ford Model T as he does behind the wheel of his racing Marmons or Cadillac convertible.

Every room displays more of the same, attesting to the fact that Mook is a career bachelor. Most homes would have a family portrait or a landscape painting above their living room fireplace, but Mook has the grille from a car he designed, the Mustang II. About that car (which is often discounted for not being a "true" Mustang) Mook insightfully notes, "It was the right car for that time. And we sold a lot of them."

With light streaming in the large glass patio door, the view from behind Mook's studio drawing board is simply beautiful. The sunlight reflects across the surface of the lake and provides inspiration and relaxation for the work that Mook continually has in process. Mook still has many more cars than he has room for at his lake house, but it's a situation he's content with. We all should be so fortunate. ◆

Chapter 9
THE GENERAL'S GARAGE

GARAGE OWNER:

GENERAL MOTORS HERITAGE CENTER

Photography by Bobby Alcott & Rex Roy

A full-time risk-taker and part-time industrial savant, Billy Durant formed General Motors in 1908. He created the corporation by merging existing companies, most of which continued to operate independently with only loose management from the top. During Durant's storied career, he lost control of the company, won it back, and then lost it all for good. But regardless of who was running General Motors, even into the 1970s, the corporation's divisions continued to operate with the autonomy that Durant originally encouraged.

So what? This is a book about garages not business management. Exactly. But understanding GM's history makes the accomplishments of the General Motors Heritage Collection that much more impressive. What Greg Wallace, manager of the collection, and his team have managed to assemble is historically significant, not only for General Motors, but for the auto industry itself.

To hear Wallace tell it, "GM's divisions pretty much did their own thing. There was no corporate-wide effort to save important vehicles or artifacts." Like many companies, GM didn't spend much time looking back, because their future lay in the opposite direction on the timeline. That truth aside, Wallace explained how many items were saved, "Historical preservation was the work of passionate individuals within divisions: Pontiac, Buick, Chevrolet, GMC, Oldsmobile, and Cadillac. People saved things at factories or in warehouses—wherever they could—because they knew one day it would be important to have them."

Things changed in the 1990s as GM flirted with bankruptcy and instituted a number of sweeping organizational changes. In an oversimplification of the restructuring,

The GM Historical Collection comprises approximately 800 vehicles. Its display building has room for 200 to 230 vehicles within its 81,000 square feet. Vehicles on display change frequently, as cars and trucks are routinely loaned to museums or used for promotional purposes.

Previous Spread: The staff at the General Motors Historical Collection knew we were coming and placed a pristine periwinkle 1958 Chevrolet Impala on the display pad in front of their main building. Without a vehicle in front, it is easy to pass this building by since it looks like just another big brick box in an industrial park.

the vehicle divisions were no longer independent. Operating functions that were once the responsibility of the divisions (e.g., vehicle design and engine production) were handed over to centralized management, design, engineering, and production groups. An unexpected result of this move was that the corporation noticed its history, and the fact that no one was charged with preserving it. Thus the General Motors Heritage Collection came to be in June 2004.

Located in a ubiquitous industrial park not thirty-minute's drive from the General Motors world headquarters in downtown Detroit, the collection occupies a tidy but otherwise mundane brick building. On display within the 81,000-square-foot facility is a journeyman's try at presenting the history of the world's largest automobile corporation. The task is harder than one might imagine because, since 1908, General Motors has produced innu-

merable models—thousands and thousands of unique vehicles on three continents. Wallace oversees the care of approximately 800 cars and trucks. Only a quarter of the collection can be accommodated at the main facility we visited, so the balance is stored in nearby warehouses.

Wallace was one of the individuals who fought to preserve the history of the division he worked for, Cadillac. In 1986, he and a team of dedicated employees succeeded in securing approval and a budget to preserve the Cadillac division's history. For more than a decade, it was the only such group in existence within General Motors. To hear Wallace tell it, his job of putting together Cadillac's historical collection was far easier than compiling all of GM's history, "Cadillac stayed on Clark Street (in Detroit) for so long, that lots of great cars and pieces were right there just waiting to be put together in a collection. We just had to officially take responsibility for them. What we didn't have, we looked for.

No garage is complete without the proper signage. The GM's Heritage Collection displays a mix of original and restored neon, as well as reproductions the collection recreated from original plans. The cars in the foreground are past show vehicles used to generate positive press.

Heading up a long line of small cars is the 1963 Corvair Super Spyder. This radically restyled Corvair looks something like the racing Corvettes that had been campaigned under the direction of GM's Zora Duntov. Behind the Super Spyder is an electric-powered Corvair, the Electrovair II. Behind this row, it's easy to spot classic Chevrolets from the 1950s, a Nomad and a Bel Air.

Looking over the hood and fender of a 1915 Chevrolet, you see three Chevys that helped General Motors control more than half of the U.S. car market in the 1960s. Under the hood of the 1969 Kingswood Estate Wagon in the background is a Central Office Production Option (COPO) 425-horsepower Turbo-Jet 427-cubic-inch big-block V-8. The Camaro is a 1967 SS Indy Pace Car replica. The Malibu (right), is an SS powered by a 289-cubic-inch small-block V-8.

Sandwiched between a perfect second-generation Corvette and a customized Chevrolet pickup are two of the most common Chevrolets of the 1970s: the Chevette and the Caprice Classic. The little Chevette is a Bicentennial Edition that has never been titled. The Caprice was titled and proudly displays the crushed velour interior, wire hubcaps and padded landau vinyl roof that the original owner ordered.

Proudly leading the collection of Buicks is the world's first pure concept car, the 1938 Buick Y-Job. Designed by the acclaimed team from Harley Earl's Art and Colour Studio, the Y-Job was used to evaluate certain design themes Earl hoped to bring to production. The Y-Job featured hidden headlamps, integrated fenders, and a raked windshield.

Some things we found at other Cadillac plants, others we purchased from collectors or at auction."

Wallace's technique worked for Cadillac and is now applied to the entire GM Heritage Collection. "We already had some 'firsts' and 'lasts' when it comes to production models." He is referring to vehicles such as the last production Cadillac Cimarron from 1988 and the final bustle-back Seville from 1986. "We're also making sure we acquire examples of important models as they come off the line." Wallace then talks about a first-generation Saturn they have on display, plus a first-generation Hummer H2 SUT and a 2002 fourth-generation Pontiac Firebird—all in what is clearly the greatest collection of General Motors vehicles anywhere.

Access to the GM Heritage Collection is by invitation only. The facility's main entry is through a small, carpeted reception area, occupied during our visit by a stunning 1965 Buick Riviera. Designed by Bill Mitchell, one of GM's most flamboyant studio heads, the car's clean stance rebelled

against the overblown fins and chrome characterizing GM products from the late 1950s and into the early 1960s. As nice as this single car was, it could not begin to set the stage for what lay beyond the simple wood doors at the opposite end of the room.

These doors opened to a display area spanning almost two full acres. The feeling is not so much of a dream garage, but of a dream warehouse, with high ceilings, cement floors, and industrial lighting. Cars are parked in diagonal rows, tail-to-tail. While there are outliers, most vehicles are part of obvious groups. The Chevrolets are with other Chevrolets and Pontiacs with Pontiacs, plus groups of racing vehicles, concept vehicles, and row upon row of engines.

Immediately inside the doors, two finned cars grab your attention. Those familiar with GM's famous Motorama traveling tour from the 1950s will remember the Firebird concept vehicles. These are anything but the popular Pontiac Firebird production car introduced in 1967. Pure design exercises, the 1954 Firebird XP-21, the 1956 Firebird II, and the 1959 Firebird III gave the world a peek at engineering and styling concepts that fired the imagination.

Each Firebird is powered by a gas turbine engine—in other words, a jet. Literature of the day suggested that General Motors was testing the feasibility of commercializing turbine engines. Excitement about the emerging jet age certainly affected the automotive world at that time. These cars gave GM design chief Harley Earl just the excuse he needed to radically explore one possible direction cars of the future could take.

Only the latter two Firebirds were present during our visit, as the XP-21 was out on loan. Details of their specifications remain impressive: titanium bodies, ventilated seat cushions, adjustable pedals, zoned air conditioning, hydraulic air suspension, drive-by-wire steering, and much more.

Close to the Firebirds was a row of small cars, headlined by three Corvairs, Chevrolet's unfairly maligned rear-engined compact of the 1960s. The 1963 Corvair Super Spyder was developed by GM designer Bill Mitchell's group to show what was possible with the practical little Corvair. Clearly a Corvair, one can imagine the Super

The Firebird III is one of three General Motors concepts that truly pushed the envelope of 1950s technology. The last of the trio, the Firebird III's lightweight titanium body is powered by a gas turbine engine that is controlled in a "fly by wire" manner.

The unmistakable grille of a 1967 Pontiac GTO looks out as if the leader of the Pontiac pack. At the left, one of the first Pontiac models from 1926 stands proud, as does a 1927 model, followed by a 1956, a 1961 Tempest, a 1969 GTO, and a 1969 Firebird.

Two of the most famous Corvettes ever are the 1965 Mako Shark II (or Manta Ray) and the original 1963 Mako Shark. While the latter was a fanciful design exercise, the former hinted at what the next generation of Corvette would look like when it arrived in 1968. Various Corvettes are behind the two concepts, with the nose of a rare 1978 Silver Anniversary Indy Pace Car clearly visible.

Spyder under the lights at an auto show, with crowds of people straining for a look at the small sports car.

Just behind the Super Spyder is a vehicle just as forward-thinking, the Electrovair II. As the name implies, this Corvair is electrically powered. The electric motor occupies the space in the trunk where the discarded internal-combustion used to be. This engineering "study vehicle" ran into many of the same issues facing today's electric vehicles, including the one

the industry still battles with, the number of miles delivered by a single charge. Farther down that row were more examples of small cars from General Motors, including the once-popular Chevrolet Vega.

Across from these somewhat common cars stood a figurative legion of the most exotic Corvettes in the world. Show and concept Corvettes spanning three decades dominate the display, with one-off vehicles such as the mid-engine

As if managing approximately 800 full-size cars and trucks isn't enough, the team at the GM Heritage Collection has also gathered toys and promotional items from GM's past. In the foreground are coin banks in the form of early Chevrolet Suburbans.

AeroVette and Corvette Indy. A fourth-generation Corvette used for engineering feasibility studies sports a 12-cylinder Falconer engine. Two of the most recognizable GM concept cars ever built are included in this collection: the 1963 Mako Shark and the 1965 Manta Ray (also called the Mako Shark II). Those with an eye for Corvettes will recognize that the Manta Ray pointed directly toward the production third-generation 1968 Corvette in many ways.

"Thankfully, GM kept these concept cars," Wallace notes. "If you can believe it, many show vehicles were destroyed back in those days. Once they served their purpose on the auto show circuit, they were cut up or crushed. Those we'll never get back, but there were important production cars that we could find and add to the collection." Wallace makes this point as he walks toward a black 1957 Cadillac Eldorado Brougham. "We purchased this Eldorado fully restored. Its technology, even by today's standards, is over the top." Wallace takes his time pointing out the complex air suspension, the center-opening doors, and the power seats with a memory feature (in a time before computers, this was a significant accomplishment).

"The car was truly handcrafted and cost $13,000 at the time. And we believe GM still lost approximately $10,000 on every sale." With only 704 built, the Eldorado Brougham is among the rarest of collector cars. But when compared to other vehicles in GM's collection, many of which are one-offs, the Eldorado is comparatively common. The Eldorado is on loan from Dick Lannen whose garage is profiled in chapter 13.

"The path of least resistance is often to pitch what you don't need or can't afford to keep," says Wallace speaking from experience. "But the benefits of preserving what you can is truly worth it." Although he understands what happened over the years, he still seems to take these losses personally because so much of GM's history was simply thrown away over the decades. At one point, a person might have argued against keeping a Chevrolet Chevette, one of the division's more forgettable models. But Wallace correctly argues for the Chevette's historical place in the Chevrolet lineup and in the American car culture. The collection has a red Bicentennial edition that's never been titled and still has plastic covering the seats fitted with a red-white-and-blue commemorative fabric.

Driven 10,000 miles from their birthplace in Brazil is this pair of 1960 Chevrolet Brasil pickup trucks. The two arrived in 2005, and were added to the collection to represent the important role the Chevy pickup played in the development of Brazil's economy.

This kind of thinking is why the collection also features a plain Chevrolet Caprice, a one-time favorite of police departments and taxi companies. Seemingly more worthy are other groupings of Chevrolets, Pontiacs, Buicks, Cadillacs, and GMC trucks. Some of the most remarkable models within these clusters of vehicles include a 1967 Pontiac GTO, a 1953 Buick Skylark convertible, a 1931 Cadillac dual-windshield Sport Phaeton featuring a V-16 engine, a 1916 GMC steak truck, and a 1904 Oldsmobile "pie wagon" panel truck.

Over the years, Wallace and his team have also preserved or collected hundreds of trinkets and pieces of memorabilia. The most visible are the neon signs. "As you can imagine, businesses didn't see any reason to save their old, out-of-date neon signs, so they didn't. With a

couple of exceptions, one being the original Oldsmobile Rocket that we purchased from a dealer, we had to recreate what you see here. We had official corporate literature giving us dimensions and showing us exactly what they looked like, so we made our own." The GM Heritage Collection now offers authentic recreations of these signs for sale, with all profits benefiting the collection.

General Motors is often thought of as a corporate entity devoid of personality. In so many ways this impression is correct, but when one looks at the vehicles in the GM Heritage Center, it is easy to see the work of individuals who left a significant mark on this automotive manufacturer. Unless you are fortunate enough to be invited to a corporate or GM-marque club event, this is as close as you'll ever get to seeing the jewels of the GM Heritage Collection. ◆

Chapter 10
THE RACER'S WORKSHOP

GARAGE OWNER: **JACK ROUSH**

If you're a race fan, the man named Jack Roush needs no introduction. He is the force behind several NASCAR teams, including competitors in the NEXTEL Cup, Busch Series, and Craftsman Truck Series. If you're not a racing fan, these facts should still impress you: Roush teams and drivers have racked up hundreds of wins and claimed 24 national championships and titles in two different racing series, including 12 manufacturer's championships. Roush also earned 10 consecutive 24 Hours of Daytona sedan class championships and was personally inducted into the International Motorsports Hall of Fame in 2006.

Currently, Roush Industries acts as the lead corporate entity of multiple Roush-run endeavors. These include his main engineering and manufacturing company, a firm specializing in aviation, a European engineering and manufacturing entity, and all of Roush's racing teams. (The racing teams run under the banner of Roush Fenway Racing, recognizing that Roush is currently partnering with John Henry, owner of the Boston Red Socks and Fenway Park.) These companies generate enough business for Roush to employ more than 1,800 people in 50 facilities across North America and Europe. Not bad for a guy who launched his career by drag racing cars back in the 1960s.

Occupying more than 30,000 square feet in an industrial section of Livonia, Michigan, the exterior of the building is unremarkable—cinderblock and steel. But what's inside couldn't be more remarkable. It is truly Jack's garage. His personal cars and ex-Roush Racing cars are stored here, as are vehicles entrusted to him by manufacturers, friends, and family. It's a collection like no other on

Left: Historically significant Mustangs are parked with retired race cars, show vehicles, and cars that represent important points in Jack Roush's life and career. Toward the back of the right row of vehicles is a 1951 Ford two-door that Roush restored, he says, "as a replacement for the one I wrecked when I was sixteen [years], six weeks, and six days old."

Previous Spread: Jack Roush began unintentionally collecting cars more than 20 years ago. Today, the collection of more than 115 vehicles is managed by his daughter, Susan Roush McClenaghan. The 30,000-square-foot facility is located in Livonia, Michigan, in close proximity to several Roush Industries facilities.

Below: This 1969 Mustang anchors the Roush collection. Roush acquired the car in 1971 and restored it nearly two decades later. The limited-production Mustang is powered by the formidable Boss 429 engine, a hemi-head design that produced 375 brake horsepower.

Many of Roush's personal cars have names. This 1940 Ford five-window business coupe is named "Bob," and is the car Roush has driven cross-country several times in The Great Race competition.

the planet. The garage includes a well-equipped restoration area staffed by craftsmen who breath life back into used-up race cars and old classics.

Responsibility for the facility falls to Jack Roush's daughter, Susan Roush McClenaghan. She talks about the early days: "I've been managing the collection for about 15 years, and cars were stored in every little corner where we could find space, scattered among many different Roush facilities. Around 2000, we found that it was just too hard to manage all of our existing assets, and we were still acquiring more vehicles, many of which had value." McClenaghan recognized the opportunity to consolidate the collection when a Roush Industries vehicle production program was ending, freeing up the current building.

The collection's first vehicle came to Roush personally in 1971. He tells the story: "When I was partnered with Wayne Gapp, we were racing Ford Mavericks with Boss 429 engines. We were the ones to go to if you had a 429, and one day this kid brought us this Boss 429 Mustang. He had been racing it and had already blown the motor twice. He was in way over his head financially and offered the car to us because he was enlisting in the Navy and wanted to

Jack Roush is one of the most recognizable figures in modern motorsports. His daughter, Susan Roush McClenaghan, is no stranger to motorsports, having grown up around racers and race car builders. The two stand in front of a 1939 Ford, the car McClenaghan and her husband drive cross-country in the Great Race.

Race- and championship-winning stock cars populate Roush's garage. This particular car is a Ford Fusion driven in NASCAR NEXTEL Cup competition by Matt Kenseth.

get his life back together. We bought it for what he owed, about $1,300. I kept it for years in our family garage and then passed it off to a friend who was going to restore it, but he ended up parking it outside for 15 years. That did more damage to it than all the racing the kid ever did. Because it is only one of about 850 1969 Boss Mustangs with a 429 V-8, I finally got the car back and restored it." Roush went on to explain how Ford produced just enough models with the 429 V-8 to homologate the engine so it could be used in NASCAR. The car stands as a rare example of a truly notable and significant muscle car—an icon of Detroit iron.

Many other cars have personal significance to the Roushes. Father and daughter compete in the transcontinental rally called The Great Race. The event is restricted to historical vehicles. The senior Roush favors his 1941 Ford Deluxe military staff sedan and his 1940 Ford five-window business coupe. The female Roush prefers her 1939 Ford convertible that she drives with her husband. When asked about intergenerational competitiveness, McClenaghan responds, "Well, I've beaten him a few

Parked in what Roush calls "The Waiting Room," cars in various states of restoration wait for their completion. This shot looks over the hood of a Mustang convertible Roush personally developed and raced in the Super Stock class during the early 1970s.

Roush Industries was one of the key suppliers that helped Ford Motor Company create its acclaimed GT supercar. Roush Industries also helped DaimlerChrysler develop the Dodge Viper GTS, seen in the background.

times, and when he beats me, everybody knows. My father is a highly competitive individual."

Roush's personal competitiveness may be most clearly seen in his long racing career. Three genres of ex-racers call the garage home: stock cars, road racers, and drag cars. McClenaghan tracks current winning cars through the various teams run by Roush Fenway. She makes sure to lay permanent claim to those that earn championships and significant wins. It remains a challenge because each team fields multiple cars or trucks.

Before Roush embarked on his NASCAR assault, he was heavily involved in sports car racing. With famous drivers such as Paul Newman, Ricky Rudd, Kyle Petty, Bill Elliot, Lyn St. James, and Robby Gordon, Roush Racing has won more than 100 races. Choice examples from this period include the Mustang that won the 24 Hours of

Daytona. Roush looks out over them, rubs the brim of his signature hat, and comments, "Along the way, we've rescued any number of derelict race cars. When their useful life was done and they were ready to be scrapped, we'd save them."

Even further back in Roush's personal racing history are his drag racing cars. Two of his oldest cars are being prepped for full restorations in the garage's "waiting room." In addition to the Mustang II that Roush used to win several drag racing championships in the early 1970s, McClenaghan recently uncovered the last Super Stock car her father built, a 1969 Mustang Convertible. Of the car, Roush says, "I never thought about the car for 10 or 15 years, then the owner contacted Susan. When we contacted him, he was not a mercenary about the price, so now we've got it awaiting restoration. Because it was the last Super

This historic Mustang is a creation of Ford Special Vehicle Engineering (SVE). The 10-liter V-8 produces more than 800 horsepower that propels the car through the quarter mile in only 10.5 seconds at 135.5 mph. When SVE boss John Coletti retired in 2005, he asked Roush to be the caretaker of the car.

Stock car I built, and it won a major event in its class, it was worth saving."

Beyond significant race cars and personal vehicles, the Roush garage is home to other worthy cars. Examples of recent classics such as the Ford GT and Dodge Viper are parked there because Roush Industries played a major role in their engineering development.

Less recognizable than these production supercars, but no less interesting, are two cars that are known only by their engineering code, GN34. Ford of Europe wanted a successor to the popular DeTomaso Pantera, a sexy Italian sports car powered by an American Ford V-8 (the 351-cubic-inch Windsor). During the 1980s, Ford developed this all-wheel-drive, mid-engine coupe with

Looking somewhat nondescript, this late 1980s prototype code GN34 could have been the successor to the Ford-powered DeTomaso Pantera. Roush did much of the engine and transmission development work on the project, but the vehicle was never approved for production.

the intent of one day superseding the Pantera. The GN34 is powered by a dual-overhead-camshaft 3.0-liter engine that Ford developed with Yamaha, a Japanese manufacturer best known for its high-revving and powerful motorcycles. (Enthusiasts may recall that Ford used this engine in the well-respected first-generation Taurus SHO models.)

Roush Industries performed all of the drivetrain development for the vehicle, and several engineering prototypes were built. The bodies were fiberglass, and these particular cars used windshields and roof panels from Ferraris of the day. Unfortunately, as Ford of Europe continued to study the business case for the GN34, their financial analysis did not deem the program a wise move, and it was cancelled.

Normally in such cases the prototypes are destroyed. This action sometimes involves the vehicles being cut into pieces or having a forklift ram its skids through the body.

Roush built these vehicles as Pace Cars for the PPG Indy Car World Series. Both of these cars started life as Fox-platform Ford Mustangs.

Nestled between a turbocharged Ford Pinto and an '80s-era Mustang road racing car, this World War II–era engine is from a P51 Mustang aircraft. Roush is an aviation enthusiast, and his aviation company is one of the few companies capable of rebuilding these arcane powerplants. Customers include air racers and warbird enthusiasts.

Built for the auto show circuit, the 12-cylinder 1996 Indigo (Indy-Go) features Indy Car racing technology such as advanced aerodynamics and a monocoque chassis that incorporates carbon fiber.

A Ford Model A speedster owned by a friend of Roush's is dwarfed by a classic Hispano-Suiza that Roush's team restored for a museum in California.

Jack Roush's daughter, Susan, began her career in drag racing during the 2006 season. Her ride for the season was this Mustang equipped with a 4.6-liter V-8 modified by Roush Performance. A quick study armed with natural talent, she quickly became a force to be reckoned with.

It gets ugly. In this case, sympathetic Ford engineers working on the development team arranged to have two complete GN34s spirited off for safekeeping by Roush.

It is fitting that the GN34s are in the same garage as the much newer Ford GT. What was learned on the GN34 was used to develop the 1995 Ford GT90 show car. Experience gained on the GT90 program helped speed development of the Ford GT, first shown in concept in 2002.

While the Roush garage is not a public facility, McClenaghan notes that the company does hold special events that opens the collection to visitors. "During the summer, we like to hold events so people from car clubs and the community can see and enjoy what we have here." Information on the museum and upcoming events can be found at www.roushcollection.com.

The Roush collection mirrors Jack Roush's expansive and successful career and his love for all things automotive. The notion of family comes through, as does its unofficial role as a repository for historically significant vehicles. ◆

Chapter 11

ALL CHARGED UP

GARAGE OWNER: JAMES COUSENS

James Cousens has owned dozens upon dozens of cars. His classics have graced the fairways overlooking the Pacific at the famed Pebble Beach Concours d'Elegance and won accolades at elite gatherings such as those at Meadow Brook Hall in Michigan and on Amelia Island in Florida. Cousens used to favor the traditional American classics with names like Packard, Lincoln, Auburn, and Duesenberg. In a rather shocking change, his collection took a major turn in the early years of this new millennium.

Cousens, a major player in Michigan's construction industry, explains, "After collecting classics for years, I really thought I wanted one of everything: a four-cylinder, six-cylinder, V-8, V-12, V-16, steam-powered, electric-powered, coupe, convertible, town car, you name it. But it wasn't really possible for a guy like me to pull it off. There are just too many." Cousens continues with a smile and a wave of his arm sweeping the floor under one of his cars, "Then I got my first electric car, and I was hooked. Aside from being unusual, I got rid of all my drip trays because these cars don't leak anything."

To his knowledge, Cousens currently has the largest and most complete collection of electric vehicles in the world. Including the 7 in his residential garage, he has another 14 off-site in storage or being restored. As for the collection's name, Cedar Crossing, Cousens says, "Lots of guys name their collections after themselves. I didn't think my name would ring any bells, so I just decided to call it Cedar Crossing."

With characteristic humility, Cousens' battery-powered "phone booths on wheels" contrast dramatically with the elegant classics he previously owned. However valid the disparaging descriptor, Cousens appreciates the important

Left: When Jim Cousens built his car barn in 2004, one of his favorite vehicles was his 1930 Packard Phaeton. It became a graphic element for his collection's marquee. The rear of the Packard is featured on the sign's backside.

Previous spread: From the outside, very little gives notice that within this beautiful structure sits the largest private collection of antique electric cars in the world.

history his current cars represent. His fascination focuses on their spectrum and evolution. As he walks around the seven cars in his current "car barn," he points out evolutionary changes from the oldest to newest, "Before the turn of the century, these were really just electrified buggies. The tires were solid rubber, steering was by a tiller, and there was virtually no protection from the elements. In the first few

The entrance to Cousens' garage is on the structure's end. A single step past the thick, paneled door transports you back in time. The first vehicle you see is a completely original, unrestored 1904 Columbus Runabout. A period-correct mercury-arc battery charger sits in front of the Columbus.

Cousens' 1912 Baker Electric Special Extension Coupe once provided opulent transportation. Its black finish rivals that of one on a concert grand piano. With pneumatic tires and the "Opera Seats" cabin, the unit cost approximately $2,700. Inside, details abound and include bud vases, beautifully detailed upholstery, and an overhead net to safely transport hats.

years of the 1900s, the closed cars were very tall because they had to accommodate the fashionable hats that the wealthy wore. The height came down significantly by 1912, and even farther by the 1930s, reflecting the fashion of lower-profile hats. Like gasoline-powered cars, electrics went to pneumatic tires, gained steering wheels, and their suspensions became more refined."

His current garage is built on an attached wing of his home in Clarkston, Michigan, about 90 minutes north of Detroit. When he built the home, he thought the seven-car garage initially designed would be sufficient. Around 2003, he realized that he needed more space for his growing collection. It was then that he conceived the current space.

The rules of his subdivision helped dictate some key design characteristics, including the fact that it only has one garage door. Cousens grins as he remembers the politics and board approvals he cajoled over a long approval process, "My house already had four garage doors, and our sub stated that any one home could not have more than five garage doors. We made the one on the car barn a big one so I could drive just about anything through it." His classic Packards and Lincolns fit through the door with ease. The 90-degree angle of the door relative to the parking space in the garage presented a significant problem. Cousens commented, "Driving those old classics, they were huge and their steering was really tough. I needed a way to get those cars in the garage and get them turned."

Decked out with a fringed top and steering wheel (instead of a traditional tiller), the 1903 Columbia Electric Model XI Wagonnette was a popular city car for urban families. Batteries for the 60-volt motor were stored under the front and rear seats. Its solid rubber tires road roughly, but never went flat.

His solution came unexpectedly when a friend came across an electric-powered turntable that was being decommissioned from service at the famous Detroit AutoRama. Cousens took the turntable, sunk it in the floor of his new garage, and recovered it with beautifully patterned wood. Now he could drive his classics straight in and turn them 90 degrees with the press of a button. The rotation then enabled the vehicles to be easily repositioned.

In addition to the turntable, Cousens gave his new garage space many other notable features. The floor is concrete patterned and stained like an old-fashioned brick street. Of one particularly interesting accent, Cousens explains, "My sister works for the Oakland County [Michigan] Road Commission. In the winter, their snowplows sometimes flip up manhole covers. In the spring, they end up having a stack of them sitting around the road commission's yard. My sister invited me over to have a look, and I took eight different manhole covers. We sunk them into the floor to give the place a more authentic look." Attesting to the history of the area, the covers wear the insignias such as Detroit Edison and Detroit Water Supply. Period warehouse hanging light fixtures and antiqued paneling make the interior appear to be almost a century old.

The apparent age of the space corresponds with its contents. Cousens proudly displays one of his oldest cars, a 1904 Columbus, closest to the garage's front door. Remarkably, the vehicle is totally original. While looking fragile, it is complete, right down to the beveled glass opera windows sewn into the leather top. The Columbus also features leather fenders, a weight-saving feature utilized on electric vehicles through the 1920s.

The Queen Victoria Brougham by Chicago's Woods Motor Vehicle Company is the only remaining example of a 1905 Model 120 known to exist. Its all-wood body is actually a convertible. An all-weather brougham top fits atop a traditional open coupe. Note the height of the cabin—it accommodated the fashionable hats of the day.

The lightweight design of electrics is easily seen in the 1906 Columbia Electric MK LV III Victoria Phaeton. The fenders and curved dash are made of leather stitched over tubular steel frames. The 10-horsepower General Electric motor was powered by 24 cells and propelled the vehicle up to 17 mph. This is one of five known to remain.

In his 1922 Milburn Model 27L, Jim Cousens sits at the tiller of a type of vehicle that he thinks may foretell the future of the automobile. The electrification of America was not completed in time to prevent the demise of these first-generation electric vehicles. Times have changed.

Looking somewhat like a machine Dr. Frankenstein would hook up to a just-sewn-together monster, Cousens procured a period-correct mercury-arc battery charger to go with the Columbus. The huge collection of wires and tubes connect a home's alternating-current power source to the direct-current batteries of the electric car. A full charging cycle took about eight hours. Today, the same task is performed by a device not much larger than a hard-covered book in as little as two hours. Cousens has replaced all the original Edison cells in all of his cars with modern deep-cycle golf cart batteries.

One of the newest electric vehicles in Cousens' collection is this 1931 Detroit Electric Model 97. It represents one of the last electric cars mass produced in the era. Gasoline-powered cars were becoming easier to drive and offered far greater range with quicker refueling.

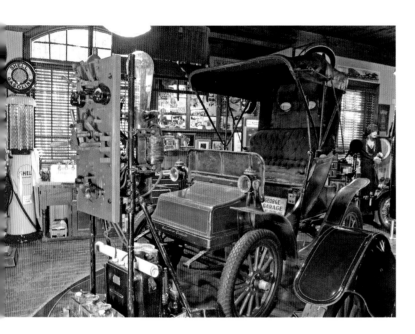

A period-correct mercury-arc battery charger sits in front of the 1904 Columbus. With multiple switches, gauges, and the big mercury bulb, it looks ready to power up a Frankenstein monster. When an electric vehicle was purchased back in the day, the new owner needed a way to charge the car's Edison 6-volt batteries (sitting on the base of the charger), and this was it.

A longtime resident of the area, Cousens found a turn-of-the-century photograph taken in downtown Clarkston, Michigan, and made it a major focal point of one garage wall. Radiator caps share space with license plates and awards conferred on classic cars Cousens previously owned.

Cousens remarks, "All of this stuff is really rare. When the cars fell out of favor, not only were the cars scrapped in huge numbers, but everything that supported them was junked, too. I bought the Columbus from a family that had owned it for 45 years, and it's the only one we know that has survived."

Another lone survivor is the remarkable Woods Motor Company electric from 1905. This Style 120 rides on a 73-inch wheelbase, and as equipped would have cost more than $3,000 new, or more than $60,000 today. Part of the extravagant cost came from the car's convertible design. Like modern generations of Corvettes and Mercedes SL roadsters, the Woods features a removable all-weather hardtop. The "top" on the Woods is considerably larger than what you'll find on a Corvette or Mercedes, however. The glass and wood structure weighs hundreds of pounds and rests on five stout pins fitted to the standard open body. Cousens remembers, "It took five guys to place the top on that open body." In keeping with its fine finished carpentry, the cabin locks with an original brass residence-style Schlage deadbolt.

One of Cousens' favorites is his 1903 Columbia Electric Model XI Wagonnette. "Wealthy guys would buy these for their wives to drive around town," Cousens says. In those days, gasoline-powered cars were dangerous to start, noisy, dirty, and complicated to drive because of their multiple controls for spark and throttle. Electric cars were safe, quiet, clean, and simple. For just these reasons, the Wagonnette was favored by urbane city types. Cousens appreciates those benefits today, but especially likes the casual elegance of the original diamond-tufted leather seats and the traditional surrey fringed roof.

Cousens has big plans for his electric car collection. On another piece of suburban Detroit property, he will soon build a museum-style space with room for at least 30 vehicles. His current garage simply can't hold the cars, signs, neon, and memorabilia that he already has. With today's renewed interest in plug-in electric vehicles, Cousens may find interest in his collection just starting to spark. ◆

Chapter 12
HOT RODS IN THE COUNTRY

GARAGE OWNER: **BILL COUCH**

When asked why he got into cars, never missing a beat, Couch countered, "Are you a psychiatrist?" After being assured there would be no fee for services rendered, he explained what in life conspired to bring him to this point, "I've often thought about how all this came together. I suppose there are more than a few contributors, but growing up on a farm is one of them. You grow up working in the fields and there's always the shop. You also live alone, not in frequent contact with a lot of other people." Couch's affable "awh shucks" nature conceals, however, the fact that he is no country bumpkin.

While his family did, in fact, live on a working farm north of Detroit, his father was part owner of a manufacturing plant that produced fasteners for the automotive industry. But this plant was not Couch's link to the automotive world. He explains, "My father had nothing to do with cars. He had no use for them. But when I was about 12 years old, this would have been about 1950, I discovered that Utica, Michigan, drug store had hot rod magazines. I'd get an allowance every week, and I couldn't wait until after dinner to go down to the store to agonize over which magazine I'd buy. So I started reading them and I saved them all, living vicariously through the magazines."

During one of Couch's trips to his town's corner drug store, he purchased the inaugural issue of *HONK!* magazine, a small-format rag on hot rods. On the cover was a handsome 1934 Ford coupe built by Joaquin Arnett. Arnett was a respected builder at the time and a member of the Bean Bandits, a light-hearted group of Hispanic racers who acquitted themselves quite well on drag strips and dry lakebeds (the team achieved some 200 world speed records over the years). Couch fills in some more details, "When I

Above: Bill Couch's 1934 Ford is one of the most recognized hot rods in the world. Known as the Granatelli Coupe, it was first created by Joaquin Arnett, and then further modified by motorsports legend Andy Granatelli. Couch purchased the car off a used car lot in 1953.

Right: While the suburbs are closing in, Bill Couch's home is still in "the country" about an hour north of Detroit. He says, "I built the barn to look like a regular outbuilding so it wouldn't attract any attention."

Previous spread: Couch's garage space is split into two sides. The finished side holds memorabilia, an impressive collection of magazines, and eight cars.

was a kid, I had a chalkboard in my room, and I put that magazine cover up on my chalkboard."

Couch didn't think much more about that car until he took a trip to Chicago to visit a friend a few years later. The story continues, "So we're out driving around in my friend's mother's car, and we saw that car, the Granatelli Coupe, sitting in the back of a Chicago used car lot. It just so happened that my friend's father was the largest Lincoln-Mercury dealer in Chicago, so he called my father to offer to check out the car." Couch did

not expect his conservative father to approve the purchase of what was then just a used hot rod with a history of hard use. But in October 1953, the senior Couch approved the purchase, and a very young Bill Couch bought the Granatelli Coupe as his first car. In 2001, Couch would display his famous coupe on the fairway alongside other significant cars of the era at the prestigious Pebble Beach Concours d'Elegance.

In the process of restoring the Coupe, Couch tracked down both Arnett and Granatelli to ask them about the

Couch purchased the 1929 Model A touring car before finishing college in Arizona and brought it to Michigan in 1961. His sons are helping him restore it. The 1914 Model T was also a Couch family restoration project, with help from friends who regularly come by the barn on Wednesday nights.

Sans paint, the 1963 Shelby Cobra shows off its lightweight aluminum body. Close observation shows that the man behind the Cobra, Carroll Shelby signed his progeny (CSX #2186 with a 289-cubic-inch V-8) when he happened across the car at a show.

car. Couch rediscovered the car's history: Arnett built the car in 1950 with the intention of selling it to earn some cash for the Bean Bandits. The car was originally black, with a convertible top and a tired-out Ford flathead V-8. Andy Granatelli, long recognized as a leader in the world of racing and high-performance automobiles, purchased the car in 1951 and took it back to Chicago where he was promoting motorsports events at Soldier's Field. Further modifications were made to the coupe under Granatelli's direction, including replacing the car's soft-top with a hardtop, the installation of a Granatelli-designed and -built racing V-8 engine, and improvements to the chassis.

Couch recounts what he did once he drove the car home from Chicago in the winter of 1954, "I just went nuts. I drag raced the hell out of that thing. In the summer I was on Woodward seven days a week. That car was really fast. But, I finally got serious about school and college, so the car just sat around the farm while I was away. The 16-inch front wheels were the same size as the hay wagon, so those went missing. And I had left the hood up on the car, and the barn leaked, so the engine froze up." The neglect continued until Couch was out of school, had gotten successful in business, and nearly finished raising his family. The Coupe's restoration started in the 1990s, and was completed about eight years later due to a couple of bad experiences with different restoration providers.

About the other cars in the garage, Couch says, "They just kind of stacked up over time because I was working so hard and raising a family." The garage is divided into two areas, one that's heated and one that isn't. Parked in the storage-oriented side is an unlikely combination of vehicles. A huge four-door catches your eye immediately. The unmistakable Rolls Royce grille topped by the Spirit of Ecstasy looks completely out of place amid the jumble of 1930s-era Ford fenders, home building materials, tractor parts, and a big kerosene heater. Officially, the Rolls is a

1931 P2 AJS Series with a sports salon body by Brewster. Couch had always wanted a Rolls Royce, and the price was right for this one. He and his family have racked up thousands of miles enjoying its superior engineering and stately performance.

Alongside the Rolls sits a 1932 Ford that looks like it was made from junkyard parts. That's because it (just about) was. The proper classification for the car in today's parlance is "Rat Rod." Couch explains, "I bought the car not long after I started college in Tucson, it would have been 1957. I turned it into a High Boy and raced it down

Extra water was essential for travel in warmer climates in decades past. At that time, and in those extreme conditions, one expected to need to add water to a car's cooling system. The bag is hung off the front of the 1914 Model T that Couch restored with his sons and friends.

Couch assembled nearly 20 complete collections of magazines such as *HONK!*, *Motor Trend*, and *Road & Track*. Dealership signs and clocks were also picked up along the way at swap meets such as the national event at Hershey, Pennsylvania.

Looking across generations of Corvettes, the wall is decorated with all manner of memorabilia, including toilet seats (a matched pair) custom painted as personal gifts to Couch by Ed "Big Daddy" Roth, the creator of Rat Fink. This red 1957 Corvette was rescued in pieces from a garage in Grosse Pointe, Michigan. Couch restored the car and often drives it in the summer. His 1978 Silver Anniversary Corvette saw summer duty for years and shows approximately 33,000 miles.

This 1968 Corvette once sat on a turntable in Cobo Hall, where it was a display car for Chevrolet during the annual Detroit Auto Show. The car is well optioned and sports a 427-cubic-inch big block.

there. I trailered it home between semesters one year, and when I went back to school, my brother decided that it was his. He put a built Chevy V-8 in it and raced it. When he moved on to another car, he yanked the Chevy out and parked my car back in the barn. Then it just sat. A couple years ago, when the people at the Detroit AutoRama started a class for Rat Rods, my sons put the car back together with extra parts we had left over from other projects. We showed the car in 2004."

More Fords are parked in the finished part of Couch's garage. Tile floors, painted walls, and a gas-fired heater make the space comfortable. Memorabilia adorns the space, including an original piece of Rat Fink art courtesy of Ed "Big Daddy" Roth. Bookcases contain complete collections of hot rod and enthusiast car magazines, including the original *HONK!* publication where Couch first saw the Granatelli Coupe. Most of the titles, such as *Road & Track,* go back more than 50 years.

Eight cars were parked in this part of the garage during our visit. Proof that his sons have picked up on his enthusiasm for cars, the white Camaro was his oldest son's high school graduation present. Beyond the Camaro is an eclectic mix. The oldest is a 1914 Ford Model T touring car. The T was a recent acquisition compared to the 1929 Ford Model A beside it. Couch purchased the Model A when he was still in college in Arizona. He recalls that he bought it from a poor Mexican family for $500, and that it ran pretty well but was missing the top and bows. He and his wife used to drive it around in the evenings to put their first son to sleep for the night. Like his other cars, it eventually ended up parked in the barn of the family farm. He and his sons are now putting the car through a full restoration.

Couch purchased his 1968 Corvette when he was actually looking for a Cobra. In his travels around Detroit, he met the first owner of a bright blue Corvette that had

Now officially classified as a Rat Rod, Couch originally purchased the car in the mid-1950s while in college in Tucson. The car was raced and customized and was most recently shown at the Detroit AutoRama.

once been a show car used on the Chevrolet stand during the 1968 Detroit Auto Show. Couch purchased it from the man, who Couch described as "the kind of guy who always needed the next newest thing. So he sold me this car, which is really well optioned, for a really good price, and it was only a year old. It became our second car, and my wife drove it for years. Even with that use, though, it only has around 35,000 miles on it. It's never been restored."

Couch continued to look for his Cobra. After the Corvette had settled into the family collection, Couch made it known that he would buy an original Shelby Cobra if the price was right. His younger son immediately started scanning the pages of *Hemming's Motor News* for a car that met his father's criteria. It happened that there was one for sale outside of Phoenix, the site of the family's

upcoming vacation for 1980. Their first full day in Arizona was spent looking at the once-red Cobra. They bought it, and called a friend back in Detroit to arrange the car's shipment home. Some old body repairs necessitated Couch's attention, and they decided that the recently refinished aluminum skin looked just fine in the raw, so they left it that way. Apparently, Mr. Carroll Shelby himself agreed, as he signed the car's nose.

As is Couch's way, when he wants a new car, he simply puts the word out. His next purchase would be a 1957 Corvette. Through his card-playing friends, his wife tracked down the car, finding it disassembled in an elderly couple's garage in the Detroit old-money suburb of Grosse Pointe. The car had been in the family since new, a gift to the family's son. While in the midst of a total restoration, the son

Today the stately 1931 Rolls Royce P2 AJS Series sees duty in parades and simple rides through the countryside surrounding Couch's farm. Approximately 100 chassis were produced by Rolls Royce for the U.S. market in 1931, with most wearing bodies by Brewster.

was tragically killed, and the car sat at the couple's home, ostensibly representing the man to his grieving parents for more than a decade. The purchase of the car took more than a year, and was finally consummated in 1978. Couch took more time than that to bring the car back to its current state.

The newest Corvette in Couch's collection is a 1978 Silver Anniversary model fitted with the high-performance L-82 engine. Unlike most of Couch's cars, this one he bought almost new. A friend who worked at General Motors purchased the vehicle using Couch's specifications, and transferred ownership to him almost immediately, a policy no-no. Some of Couch's other friends at General

Motors provided front and rear spoilers—pieces that were only available on the limited-production Indy Pace Car edition.

Outfitted as it is, Bill Couch's garage has become a meeting place of sorts for the car crazies in Detroit. Those in the community know about the open invitation on Wednesday nights. Even in winter, you can expect to find Couch and one or both of his sons in the garage chatting with other hobbyists who just stop by. Sometimes there's pizza. Often there's beer. Always there's conversation, bench racing, and plans for new projects. A guy like Couch has lots to talk about. ◆

Chapter 13
THE COMPANY MAN

GARAGE OWNER: **DICK LANNEN**

Throughout the 1950s, Dick Lannen was a Ford man. Working as a mechanic at a Ford dealer in Kenmore, New York, he dreamed of heading to Ford World Headquarters in Dearborn, Michigan. His devotion to the blue oval spilled over into his personal life as he campaigned various Fords at drag strips and on the surface streets of Kenmore and Buffalo.

As true-blue to Ford as Lannen was, certain Chevrolets caught his attention. Of course there were always Corvettes to lust after. But one evening a fuel-injected 1957 Chevrolet Bel Air shut down Lannen's Ford in a street race. He smiles as he recalls his thoughts after getting smoked, "A black '57 with fuel injection—now that would be a sweet little car." The seeds of change were sown.

Lannen knew that special access to high-performance cars came with being on the inside of companies like General Motors. As Lannen's early career progressed, one thing led to another and he hired into Chevrolet's Buffalo zone office in 1960. He would retire from General Motors 39 years later.

From the outset, Lannen made the most of his position. The story of how he came to own his first Corvette proves the point. *Route 66*, the popular TV show, was filming an episode in Niagara Falls. Responsibility for providing Corvettes for the show fell to the Chevrolet Zone Office in Buffalo. A car hauler full of new Corvettes arrived from Detroit to keep the show's crew and stars George Maharis (Buzz Murdock) and Martin Milner (Tod Stiles) happy. Lannen fell hard for the car tagged with Maharis' name. It was silver with a red interior. After the episode was produced and the production company left town, Lannen bought that car for $2,900.

"That happened in 1963," Lannen recalls. "To make it look like the upcoming '64s, the first thing I did was cut out the bar in back and replace the rear window—can you believe it?" He would never be without a Corvette again. The 1963 with the 1964 look was replaced soon after with a 1965. "And then I just kept buying newer models. I had a wife and four kids, but I always had a Corvette. We used them as everyday cars. Even my wife would drag race them—she was a good racer." He knew back then that he wanted to have a collection of Corvettes one day.

Lannen's career took off at General Motors. By 1965, he was at Chevrolet's Detroit Central Office. He progressed through positions such as district sales manager and zone manager, and by 1982 was the general service manager for Chevy. At this level of management and at each he would rise to, Lannen could have a Corvette as his company car. He also had access to leaders in the Corvette world, such as Dave McLellan, the car's chief engineer from 1975 to 1992. He also developed relationships with dealers around the country, including high-volume Corvette dealers such as Les Stanford Chevrolet in Michigan. All of these contacts would play a role in his nascent Corvette Collection.

The first car he purchased for his collection was an early production 1984, one of the first Generation IV Corvettes. It would not anchor Lannen's collection for long. Lannen's position afforded him the status of sitting on a committee that reviewed and approved future production paint colors. The Corvette that replaced his original 1984 was a second '84, but this one was painted a red destined to debut in 1986. Lannen recalls, "And it was delivered with two extra gallons of paint in the hatch just in case anything happened to it. The car was saleable, so I had my secretary contact the people at GM Design and have them tag that car for me."

As unique as this C4 Corvette was, its spot in Lannen's garage is now occupied by a 1990 ZR-1, a car so formidable that it remains in the top echelon of all performance cars. The ZR-1 gets its power from the Lotus-engineered LT5 5.7-liter V-8 that utilizes a plethora of cams, valves, and wizardry to unleash 405 SAE net horsepower through a six-speed gearbox that delivers a terminal velocity of more than 180 mph.

Lannen says that he was "too cheap" to buy a new ZR-1, so when he decided he wanted one, he put the word out to

Above: The triangular air filter conceals the Tri-Power carburetor induction system that feeds the 435-horsepower 427-cubic-inch (7.0-liter) V-8 of Lannen's 1969 Corvette. The car was a true "barn find" discovered in northern Michigan.

Previous spread: Lannen likes his Corvettes red, unless they're blue or black. The top for the 1957 hangs on the wall surrounded by framed photos that informally chronicle Lannen's career and acquisitions.

Above: Lannen took great pains to make the garage fit his property and not stick out in his established neighborhood. The brick on his new structure is a near perfect match to that on his circa-1920s Tudor home.

Twin paneled doors face the home's motor court. The home's existing attached garage opens onto the common space.

his dealer friends. Shortly thereafter, Lannen bought the "used" car pictured in this chapter with all of its original paperwork showing just 16,000 miles from one such dealer friend. While Lannen could have purchased one new, it's clear he applies Ben Franklin's adage, "a penny saved is a penny earned," to his automotive acquisitions. Wary of being accused of discarding a unique Corvette, Lannen sold the second 1984 Corvette to a major collector in Ohio, where it remains to this day.

While Lannen was trading 1984 Corvettes, he acquired his 1957 Corvette as a representative of the

model's first generation, C1 (Corvette, 1st generation). Falling back on his skills as a mechanic, he completed most of the restoration himself. "It took a great deal of time doing it piecemeal like I did, but I'm happy with what I ended up with. It's got the single headlight look that I like and the fuel-injected 283-cubic-inch engine with a four-speed and the 3.7:1 gear—the perfect combo," Lannen says.

Lannen also tried multiple times to find a C2 Corvette he could keep forever. These 1963–1967 Corvettes offered so much variety in terms of style, power, and overall refinement that Lannen had a hard time settling on what he truly wanted. Today, though, he is convinced that his fuel-injected 1965 is the ultimate second-generation Corvette. "It's got big-block power, the drivability and throttle response that come with fuel injection, better handling because of the lighter weight small block, beautiful styling, and a refined interior. It's smooth driving, but goes like hell—far superior to the original '63 in every way." Lannen then quips with a smile, "Plus, because it's a '65, it's affordable. The '67s were priced out of my budget."

This career GM man now owned a Corvette from the model's first, second, and fourth generations. He needed to fill the C3 void. "I really wanted a '69 because their quality was so much better than the '68s. And in 1970 the engines were down on power because of new emissions regulations," Lannen explains.

He found the car in a barn in Traverse City, Michigan (about four hours north of Detroit). It was a true barn find, showing only 26,000 miles. This Corvette was a 1969 that featured the 435-horsepower version of the venerable

Sitting upon his old desk from General Motors (purchased when GM modernized its interior décor) is a 1957 Eldorado Brougham. Lannen owns the vehicle that was used to create this model, and it is on loan to the GM Heritage Collection.

Lannen opines that his 1965 is the best second-generation Corvette ever built. He sites the 1965's fuel injection, improved suspension, and more refined interior. The car was so comfortable that back in the day, he used to pack his family into one for trips from Detroit to New York to visit family.

The poster at the left features Lannen's 1957 Corvette, while the photo on the right captures his 1957 Eldorado Brougham. The image was taken after the Cadillac was displayed at the prestigious Meadow Brook Concours d'Elegance.

427-cubic-inch V-8 with original side-mount exhaust. Three carburetors topped the engine, and a four-speed manual backed it up. "Because of my background in service, I knew that a huge number of these 427s blew up because the valve retainers were weak. So I never even tried to start the car. I just bought it and trailered it home. The engine rebuild was about the first thing I did." The balance of the 1969's restoration was another piecemeal affair, with the interior needing not much more than a thorough cleaning.

The C5 Corvette in Lannen's collection actually found him, as opposed to Lannen searching for it. The 1998 is one of the first four production convertibles to come off the assembly line in Bowling Green, Kentucky. The fifth-generation car went into an engineering evaluation fleet that Lannen managed. He fell in love with the car and had it transferred from company ownership to his almost immediately.

Lannen's current Gen VI Corvette came to him through one of his dealer connections. The dealer purchased the car from GM's internal fleet and discovered it was something

Lannen wears an easy smile. He is as comfortable with his Corvettes as he is with people—a trait no doubt appreciated by all those he worked with at GM.

A quarter century separates the small block V-8s in the Gen IV and Gen II Corvettes. The ZR-1's LT5 features dual overhead camshafts, four valves per cylinder, and variable intake geometry to generate 405 horsepower.

The 1965 Corvette is powered by a 327-cubic-inch V-8 fed through a mechanical fuel-injection system. Lannen reports excellent drivability from his 375-horsepower code L84 "Fuelie." While Lannen keeps his cars stock, he compromised on the '65 by fitting it with radials in place of the bias ply tires. Production records indicate only 771 were fitted with the fuel-injected engine in 1965.

unique. This particular 2005 coupe was considered a reject by GM because of its color, a dark red. After approving the color for production, Chevrolet marketing executives decided they didn't like it after all. The executives ordered the plant to discontinue the color. Only 26 cars were painted the deep red, making it among the rarest of late-model Corvettes.

Lannen's six generations of Corvette fit snugly in his freestanding garage. Its brick, roof pitch, windows, and twin doors match the styling of Lannen's Tudor home. He was extremely conscious of local building regulations, as the Detroit suburb that Lannen calls home has an "active" building inspection program to enforce local codes. The garage's interior measurements are 28 feet wide by 32 feet deep.

After 39 years with the General, Lannen is enjoying an active retirement. Look for him and his rare Corvettes at local and national gatherings from Detroit to Bowling Green. ◆

Chapter 14
OF CARS AND TRAINS

GARAGE OWNER: **RICHARD KUGHN**

Richard Kughn is perhaps Detroit's best-known car collector, and he has been for decades. A successful fixture in Detroit, Kughn's public automotive face included the operation of his Carail Museum, a 45,000-square-foot private play space. Fueled by his success in real estate, leading the Taubman Company and then working independently, his collection kept growing. In 1974, Kughn found a location in Allen Park, Michigan (just south of Detroit), to store his toys.

Throughout the next 25 years, the storage and display space grew, expanding from the small office building Kughn first purchased to the empty bowling alley next door and then the adjacent Oldsmobile dealership. The expansion stopped at 45,000 square feet and included approximately 250 classic cars and an unrivaled model train collection. It would have been hard to compete with Kughn when it came to collecting model trains, as he owned Lionel Trains from 1986 to 1995. While Kughn never opened his Carail museum to the public, he made it available by appointment and for special corporate events and charity conferences.

What is pictured here is Kughn's pared down collection. The bulk of the Carail holdings were auctioned in 2003 after Kughn, then 73, recovered from a life-threatening illness. When asked today about the auction, Kughn smiles and responds, "Well, I just wasn't getting any younger, and we just had so much stuff that wasn't being enjoyed. We thought an auction would be a good way for these things to find good homes. But it was tough. Letting go of some of those cars was like selling my children!" With about 35 cars still in his collection, plus several more at his home in Florida, Kughn still has many of his "children" around to enjoy.

Leading a string of cars that includes a 1949 Chrysler Town & Country and a 1938 Packard Rollston Town Car, Kughn's 1942 Packard Darrin 180 Victoria Convertible looks positively regal.

Previous spread: Kughn's collection is divided between his Carail warehouse and a workshop. The warehouse is a considerable step down from the 45,000 square feet and 250 vehicles Kughn once had, but the present collection remains impressive. Kughn favors convertibles and is an avid University of Michigan fan.

To say that Kughn is a collector understates his status dramatically. Curiously, he thinks his condition may have started with soap. "I think soap was my first collection," said Kughn. "About 1937 or '38. They were little figures of soap: the Lone Ranger, Tonto, Snow White, and Mickey and Minnie Mouse. I kept them on a shelf. I loved them," said the man whose passion for gathering resulted in one of the largest collections in the United States, if not the world.

Trains would come next, beginning at age seven. Cars were not far behind. Kughn easily remembers his first car, "It would have been 1947, and I was walking home from high school one day with one of my buddies. We were talking about not having any wheels, and we decided that we could try building a car from junkyard parts. So we did. Now, we did it with proper junkyard parts to wind up

with a complete 1923 Model T touring car. I drove that car all during my senior year in high school and had a ball with it. That got me hooked on what you start to see here in this collection."

Currently, Kughn's collection is housed in two facilities, a workshop and a warehouse. Our tour started in the workshop where the manager, Bob Ferrand has been restoring and maintaining the collection for more than 20 years. Ferrand outfitted the workshop with necessary tools of the restoration trade, including hoists, welding equipment, and paint booth.

Since the space is just a workshop, the cars are simply parked in a line with no particular thought given to a proper presentation. This didn't stop many of the cars from standing out as excellent examples of their genre. Perhaps the most noteworthy is the dark blue 1942

Epitomizing success and civic pride, Richard Kughn's affable presence makes conversation easy. His collection reveals a genuine appreciation for the historical progress of automotive design and technology.

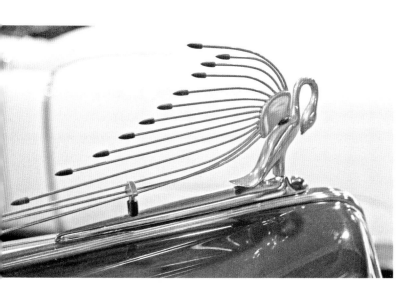

Proudly displaying its metallic plumage atop a 1942 Packard Darrin, the marque's mascot (the Cormorant) does double duty as a hood ornament and a radio antenna.

Packard Darrin Victoria Convertible. Kughn explains, "This was actually the very last Packard Darrin convertible ever built, and it was built for Gene Autry." For those non-Hollywood types, Autry was the world's most famous singing cowboy, and his career in film, radio, and television spanned nearly 70 years.

As he walks through his four-wheeled family, Kughn continues to explain where his affinity (sometimes revealed as outright affection) comes from, "I love the art of the automobile, and the history of the development of the automobile. Every car represents a swath of the world of transportation of four wheels. That's what drives my passion for the hobby."

Other milestone cars in the workshop include his matched pair of 1953 General Motors vehicles. One is a Cadillac Eldorado Convertible and the other is a Buick Skylark Convertible. Both were line-topping halo cars for their respective divisions and were significantly different from other Cadillacs and Buicks of the day. Records from General Motors indicate that only 532 Eldorados and 1,690 Skylarks were built. Kughn believes these cars epitomize the reign of GM Art and Colour Studio chief Harley Earl.

Another car from General Motors represents an important bit of automotive technology. The 1941 Series 75 Cadillac Fleetwood Sedan is one of two known to remain in the world. Its claim to fame is that it was the first car from General Motors produced with factory air conditioning. Kughn notes, "It was truly a modern marvel, and when you turn that blower up, it will freeze you right out." Necessarily an expert on such things, Ferrand pointed out that Packard beat GM to the market with A/C by one year, but the technology needed more time to mature before the public would accept it *en masse.*

Showing Kughn's keen appreciation for details is a humble 1936 Plymouth convertible. The car is the most heavily accessorized vehicle in the workshop, boasting two spare tires, plus dual horns, fog lamps, spotlights, rear wheel skirts, a trunk, and a rumble seat. Standing among elegant and stately Cadillacs and Packards, Kughn opines that, "This car is without a doubt the sexiest car in the garage. It's just such a great example of classic elegance. It's just a sweetheart of a car." Obviously, to Kughn, if you're going to have a Plymouth, this is the one.

With a stance considerably lower than other 1953 Cadillac models, the limited-production Eldorado Convertible figuratively dripped with style. Its wraparound windshield and custom-made hood, cowl, doors, and trim (by craftsmen at Fisher/Fleetwood) made the car distinctive.

The 1953 Skylark was an anniversary car celebrating 50 years of Buick. While there were some parts common to other Buick models, Skylarks were essentially custom built by the factory, delivering a lower, sportier, and more elegant automobile.

Elegant from any angle, this 1941 Cadillac 75 Series Fleetwood Sedan carries a rare factory option: air conditioning. Nineteen forty-one was the first year that General Motors offered the now commonplace feature. A large vent mounted behind the rear seats blows the cooled air forward.

Many of the cars in Kughn's collection are very well optioned, with this humble 1936 Plymouth leading the pack. Kughn says, "Without a doubt, this is the sexiest car in the garage. It's just such a great example of classic elegance." Note the car's dual horns, fog lamps, and rear wheel skirts.

Statements of style, Kughn owns two Chrysler Town & Country models, a 1948 four-door sedan and a 1949 convertible. Their hand-fitted wood exterior and interior trim showcase the craftsmanship of that bygone era.

Beautiful details highlight the fluid lines of Kughn's 1960 Eldorado Biarritz Convertible. The car is original with the interior showing a pleasant patina of careful use through the decades. Under the huge hood sits an equally huge 390-cubic-inch V-8 with three two-barrel carburetors.

Kughn's 1952 Hudson Hornet Convertible was a real runner in its day. Its lightweight unibody and large in-line six-cylinder bested the performance of the day's comparable V-8 sedans.

While Kughn's daily driver is a Maybach 57, his collectible cars see the light of day and get exercised during the concours season. Kughn and his wife are frequent attendees at the nation's most prestigious events, including Amelia Island, Meadow Brook, and Pebble Beach.

A short drive from Kughn's workshop is a smaller version of his former Carail museum. Vestiges of that museum remain as the side walls of the warehouse are stacked 10 feet high with boxes of Lionel trains, antique toys, and other items that hold special places in Kughn's life. The cars remain the stars, however, and run the gamut from true classics to nearly contemporary—if 1964 is your version of contemporary.

He gravitates toward his favorites, including the 1941 Cadillac 62 Series convertible sedan. This is simply the White House car. The car was owned by the government during the Roosevelt and Truman administrations, and it was most famously used as Eisenhower's parade car when the general returned from the European theater of World War II. Kughn purchased the piece of history years ago and it was restored in his own shop. Kughn adds, "We have newspaper clippings from the day that show Eisenhower in the car. And we've done everything we can to make it as authentic as possible, right down to the five-star general's flag."

Another favorite is a 1960 Cadillac Eldorado Biarritz Convertible. Some 20 feet in length, the shape is very long and very low. Elegant, tapered fins are a highlight of the design that is motivated by a 390-cubic-inch V-8 topped with three two-barrel carburetors. Showing fewer than 50,000 miles, everything on the car is original, right down to the carpeting.

Kughn's all-original 1964 Lincoln Continental shows an evolution of luxury car design. With the dawn of the 1960s, radical fins and the garish use of chrome went the way of the Studebaker. The pillarless design of the Continental still stands out today as one of the cleanest automotive shapes ever. Ferrand demonstrated the operation of the convertible top during our tour. The antique mechanicals buzzed and whirred to reverse open the trunk lid that revealed a space that swallowed the top, leaving only a clean rear deck showing. The new retractable hard-tops of today have nothing on this car.

Among the more stately vehicles in Kughn's collection is the 1940 Packard 8 with a convertible sedan body custom built by Derham in Pennsylvania. Packard aficionados may note the resemblance between this 180 Series and the bodies used on smaller 160 Series cars. In the process of fully restoring the vehicle more than 25 years ago, it was found that the coachbuilder stretched a 160 Series convertible sedan body to fit the larger 180 Series car. The result is a genuinely unique Packard.

Kughn is a big fan of the University of Michigan. Designed to make a real entrance when attending games at Michigan's Big House, Kughn and collection curator Bob Ferrand completed a visual makeover on the otherwise ordinary 1948 Dodge sedan.

Known as the White House Cadillac, this 1941 Cadillac 62 Series Convertible Sedan provided transportation for Presidents Roosevelt and Truman and was used as a parade car for General Eisenhower upon his successful return from the European Theater.

The Limited Convertible was actually the most expensive Buick one could buy in 1958. Legend has it that it also wore more chrome trim than any other car. Ever. Its Nailhead V-8 is matched to a sophisticated automatic transmission with an ultra smooth shifting variable stator torque converter.

Many cars built prior to World War II featured chassis produced by a manufacturer that carried bodies produced by a coachbuilder. The Derham Company custom built this one-of-a-kind convertible sedan that is fitted to a Packard 180 Series chassis.

The contrast between the bombastic finned 1950s models and the cleaner design of the mid-1960s is clearly demonstrated by comparing the rear profiles of a 1958 Buick Limited and a 1964 Lincoln Continental.

Kughn's wife, Linda, also has a favorite car in the collection, a beautiful black cherry 1948 Lincoln Continental Convertible. Besides being an icon of beautiful American design (thanks to the efforts of Edsel Ford), Ferrand pointed out some of the car's innovative engineering solutions. The power top mechanism and side windows are hydraulically operated, while the power antenna, windshield wipers, and washer jets are vacuum powered. By his own admission, the varied solutions that

different manufacturers utilized over the years to accomplish similar tasks keeps Ferrand sharp as he maintains the collection. He considers his position and comments, "I could have been a tech and worked on new cars, but I didn't want to be a guy who just switched parts in and out. I like to learn about the cars and be smart about keeping them running."

Among the other cars in Kughn's collection that includes stunning Pontiacs, Hudsons, Mercurys, and

Reaching back to a more classic era of automobiles and motoring, one of the oldest cars in Kughn's collection is his elegant Lincoln Dual Cowl Phaeton from 1931.

Oldsmobiles, one particularly stands out: the neo-classic he created with the famous designer, Gordon Buehrig. In the 1920s and 1930s, Buehrig penned many designs for premium manufacturers such as Cord, Auburn, and Duesenberg. He and Kughn became friends later in Buehrig's life, and one evening when Kughn was at Buehrig's home for dinner, he spotted a drawing on the master's drawing table. Kughn fell for the design, and committed to build it. Long-term liability issues (thank you Association of Trial Lawyers of America) prevented the design from going into full production, but three were completed. The construction is all hand-laid fiberglass over a third-generation Chevrolet Corvette chassis that was lengthened 22 inches.

Standing back to look over his more modest collection, Kughn generalizes, "It really depends on your age as to what kind of cars you like. I was born in 1929, and my collection reflects when I grew up and what strikes my fancy. These cars have memories for me, and they all express a work of art as how the cars progressed through the decades." Even as he nears 80, it is clear that Kughn will remain active and do more buying and selling. His love for all things automotive seems just as strong as it was when he was a teen, building that first Ford Model T. ◆

While not nearly as popular as the 1955 Chevrolet, Kughn likes this 1955 Pontiac Star Chief Convertible. He owned a similar car almost 50 years ago, and it was his first convertible.

Chapter 15
MYSTICAL MOPARS

GARAGE OWNER: **HAROLD SULLIVAN**

Photography by Bobby Alcott

There are men who swear by Fords. Other men revere cars from General Motors. Less common are those expressing an allegiance to Chrysler products. These individuals appreciate Chrysler's perennial underdog status and respect the innovation and tenacity that helped the smallest of Detroit's old Big Three produce some of the world's most recognizable and respected cars—especially the muscle cars.

Often called Mopars, Chrysler products run the gamut from mundane to magical. The vehicles in Harold Sullivan's garage in Madison Heights, Michigan, are so exceptional that they border on unbelievable. But they are not apparitions. Each one is simply the rarest of the rare, featuring powertrains and options and colors that are exceedingly special. Several are truly unique vehicles, each being one-of-a-kind from the factory. Sullivan has spent 17 years collecting and restoring various cars, and now owns the preeminent collection of Chrysler muscle cars in the world.

To walk through the collection is to enter a world of what ifs, as in, "What if I bought that car in 1978 for $3,500. I'd be a millionaire now." You see vehicles that may have once been for sale in your town's local newspaper, as many of these cars were just unloved used cars in the late 1970s. Sullivan has the knack for tracking down and then restoring some of the most valuable Chrysler products on the planet.

One of Sullivan's greatest acquisitions is known the world over as the Silver Bullet. Ask any man who cruised Woodward Avenue, and he'll know the legend of the Silver Bullet. The lore was that this 1967 Plymouth Belvedere was clandestinely supported by Chrysler and the engineers from the high-performance Direct Connection parts program. With special prototype factory racing parts and

The legendary Silver Bullet (left) was a real car that prowled Woodward Avenue in search of prey to trounce. Once a factory test car, Sullivan tracked the icon down from a civilian owner. Too valuable to continue driving, Sullivan built a near clone to race, the Silver Bullet II (right).

Previous spread: Harold Sullivan's garage may contain more Mopar Muscle than any other single space on earth. With the exception of his limited-production V-10-powered Dodge Ram SRT-10, every old Chrysler Corporation vehicle in Sullivan's collection is powered by a 440-cubic-inch "wedge" or 426 Hemi engine.

dozens of clever modifications, the Silver Bullet was never beaten in a street race. This was an amazing feat given the fierce competition of the era, when engineers from Ford and General Motors routinely tested factory-tuned high-performance models on the street. Sullivan has timing slips proving that the car is capable of running the quarter mile in 10.3 seconds with a trap speed of more than 135 mph.

After the car was used as a test mule by Chrysler, it was sold to a local mechanic, Jimmy Addison, who continued to informally campaign the car on Woodward. As stricter law enforcement, emissions regulations, and stifling insurance rates killed off the muscle car, the Silver Bullet disappeared. Through one of those wonderful flukes of life, a mechanic who Sullivan hired to maintain his fleet happened to know the owner of the legendary Plymouth. Sullivan inquired, and as often happens in sales or trades of important vehicles, much time passed before anything came to be. When the buyer finally agreed to sell, the payment was not money, but another rare Chrysler. Sullivan recalls, "He didn't want any money, but he knew I might be able to find a car he wanted. He asked me to find him a 1970 Plymouth Superbird in Petty Blue with a white interior. That's a rare car itself, but I tracked one down in Ohio. It was a really good car, and once I got it up to my shop, we did the trade. That's when the restoration on the Silver Bullet started. After being underground for almost two decades, the car was coming back."

Chrysler knew how to get the market's attention, and color was one way. The 1970 Plymouth Road Runner (left) is one of only nine known to exist and is painted a bright Lemon Twist. The same year Plymouth model (right) is the only GTX 440 Six Pack ever painted Moulin Rouge from the factory.

As is Sullivan's way, he tracked down engineers who worked on the Silver Bullet, as well as Jimmy Addison. The information Sullivan gathered helped his team restore the car to the condition it was in when it reigned as King of Woodward Avenue. The stroked 426-cubic-inch Hemi (displacing 487 cid) was rebuilt, and the lightweight fiberglass body panels were refinished. Everything is period correct.

When Sullivan debuted the restored GTX, the muscle car community went wild. Magazines from Germany, Sweden, Japan, and the United States featured the Silver Bullet. Sullivan says, "After I got it done, I really wanted to race it. But I just couldn't modify it. Putting roll bars in and tubbing it out would have been wrong, so I just built a clone. That's the Silver Bullet II, and that's the one I race. It's a Hemi, too, making about 1,000 horsepower. I've run a 9.17 quarter in it at 152 mph. I get out in it four or five times per year, and run it at all the big events."

Some of Sullivan's cars are too perfect or too valuable to drive at all. In addition to his many rare Plymouth Road Runners and GTXs, there are the extraordinarily valuable

Special ordered for a customer in Germany, this 1971 Charger is one of a kind. It raced across northern Europe by its owner, a U.S. serviceman. The Charger awed crowds with its rare 426 Hemi engine and set records with its fearsome performance.

The 1969 Dodge Daytona (left) and 1970 Plymouth Superbird (right) were called Mopar's Winged Warriors. Designed to win in NASCAR events with superior aerodynamics, the cars were so successful they were legislated out of competition. Both of Sullivan's examples are Hemi-powered.

The Superbird's aerodynamically contoured nose is grafted onto what is essentially a two-door 1970 Plymouth Belvedere. After a partial build at the Chrysler Lynch Road plant, the cars were hand-finished at Chrysler's Clairpointe Assembly facility. The nose adds 19 inches to the body and a stabilizing down force at more than 90 mph.

E-Bodies. Built off of a common platform, the 1970–1974 Dodge Challenger and Plymouth 'Cudas are hot commodities, especially when equipped with high-performance options. Sullivan has plenty of them. When Sullivan began collecting Mopars, he reasoned, "The 440 Six Pack and Hemi cars didn't cost that much more to buy than a regular 440 Magnum car or one with a 383. They all cost about the same to restore, so I figured I'd focus on restoring only the best cars I could find. The extra effort has paid off, especially with the Hemi cars." The result of this logic is obvious, as every car in Sullivan's collection is powered by a 440-cid engine with three two-barrel carburetors (a Six Pack) or a 426 Hemi. Sullivan provides an interesting bit of Mopar trivia, "Chrysler introduced the 440 Six Pack midyear in 1969, and they discontinued the option after 1971. That makes it a very rare combination, even rarer than the Hemi in a lot of cases."

Among the gems in his collection, Sullivan points to his 1970 Challenger R/T with the SE package. The SE was a luxurious trim package that added a vinyl roof and leather seats to the pony car, and 1970 was the only year they offered the option with the smaller rear window. His is one of 60 built.

Had *Cops* been a show in 1971, Sullivan's Plum Crazy 'Cuda might have been a segment feature. The car was stolen from its Canadian owner not long after he took delivery, and simply vanished. A friend of Sullivan who lived in Canada caught wind of the 'Cuda and, with Sullivan's blessing, began looking for it 25 years after it disappeared. Sullivan continues the story, "He'd call me and tell me he found the motor or the steering column or the glass. The car had been parted out. He finally located the stripped body on an Indian reservation. We were able to buy most of these original parts, and I had been saving lots of NOS [new old stock] parts for a project just like this, so when we got the car back, I had what we needed to restore it back to what you see here." There were only 11 'Cuda Convertibles made with Hemi engines in 1971.

Even more visually arresting than Sullivan's 'Cudas and Challengers are his pair of winged Chryslers. The 1969 Dodge Daytona and 1970 Plymouth Superbird were conceived to help Chrysler's NASCAR racing efforts. To qualify the cars for NASCAR competition, the manufacturer needed to build a specified run of "for sale" production vehicles. Chrysler did. Daytonas and Superbirds were limited-production

The tail of the 1970 Plymouth Superbird is 6 feet above ground. Its height put the spoiler's airfoil in clean air, helping stabilize the car at racing speeds. Out of the factory, these cars were capable of 140 mph. Modified for NASCAR racing, they were capable of more than 240 mph. *Photo by Rex Roy.*

These 1971 Chrysler E-Body convertibles are among the most valuable muscle cars in the world. The Go Mango orange Challenger (left) runs with a 440 Six Pack while the In-Violet 'Cuda (right) has the more exclusive Hemi. A nearly identical 'Cuda sold in 2006 for $2.4 million.

Sullivan collects model cars, and like his full-size collectibles, he focuses on the highest quality and rarest models he can find. Scale models of many of his actual cars can be found on display shelves at the garage.

Several of Sullivan's 'Cudas and Challengers have the feature known as a Shaker Hood. The air scoops lead directly to the engine's carburetor, supplying them with the unrestricted flow of air needed to develop huge horsepower.

homologation specials—hand-assembled cars based on high-volume coupes. The Daytona was based on the Dodge Coronet and the Superbird on the Belvedere. Partially assembled base cars were sent to another Chrysler facility (Clairpointe Assembly) where teams finished the units with parts produced or procured by a long-time Mopar supplier, Creative Industries. Five hundred and three Daytonas and approximately 1,920 Superbirds were produced for public sale.

While the cars appear similar, almost nothing is interchangeable. However, their on-track impact was similar and immediate. At NASCAR events, the Winged Warriors devastated their Ford and Chevy competition. Superior aerodynamics of 0.28 cd (slipperier than most of today's performance cars) and Hemi power enabled the Chryslers to easily outrun the competition on the way to the checkered flag. So great was Chrysler's design advantage that in March 1970, NASCAR pilot Buddy Baker set a lap record in a Charger Daytona of 200.447 mph at Talladega Superspeedway. In typical NASCAR fashion, the organization quickly legislated rule changes that made the cars uncompetitive, but Chrysler had already made history. Baker's record stood for 13 years. This surprised no one at Chrysler, as during development, NASCAR driver Charlie Glotzbach had lapped the company's huge oval at the Chelsea Proving Grounds at a sweltering 243 mph!

Like the cars Baker and Glotzbach drove, both of Sullivan's examples are Hemi-powered and feature the preferred four-speed manual transmission. The Hemi Orange Daytona even has the ultra-rare Kelsey Hayes aluminum 15-inch wheels—very few sets remain since they were the subject of a safety recall, and most were destroyed.

Sullivan's appreciation for these Chryslers comes from growing up on the streets of Detroit, and like so many others his age, personal experiences on Woodward Avenue. He says, "My first Chrysler was a 1967 Plymouth GTX with a 440 four-barrel and an automatic that I bought used in 1968. I still remember the first time I got behind the wheel and put the pedal to the metal. The feeling of the horsepower and torque is something I'll never forget. From that day on, that's what hooked me on Mopars." Nearly 40 years later, his enthusiasm for the brand is still there. ◆

Menacing in their glossy black paint, these two Mopars each feature a 440-cubic-inch wedge motor with Six Pack induction. The older (left) is a 1970 Plymouth GTX. The younger (right) is a 1971 Plymouth Road Runner. Sullivan drives both cars during the summer months.

Being in Detroit has a way of affecting people like Harold Sullivan. He now owns one of the finest collections of Chrysler muscle cars in the world.

Chapter 16

IT'S ALL IN THE FINISH

GARAGE OWNER: **LARRY SMITH**

When the lights come on in Larry Smith's Bloomfield Hills garage, the first thing that strikes you is the vibrancy. So many collections house cars and trucks that are painted "safe" colors such as black or silver. The pallet of Smith's collection includes gold, deep bottle green, several shades of red and navy blue, off white, and a light green that looks like the underside of a mint leaf still on the plant. The colors draw you in to look more closely at the finishes, which at their shallowest seem a mile deep. It should come as no surprise, then, to find out that Smith is the founder and owner of Autometric Collision, the premier automotive body repair facility in the Midwest.

Once your eyes have adjusted to the colors, the second thing that strikes you is the variety in Smith's freestanding, 12-plus car garage. Some guys collect brass or classic era cars, others are just into muscle cars or hot rods or one single marque. Smith's collection contains a little bit of everything, reflecting an acceptance of all things automotive.

This state of mind should suit Smith well given one his responsibilities as chairman of the prestigious Meadow Brook Concours d'Elegance. Accepted in September 2006, Smith takes over from Don Sommer, the founder and first chairman of the Meadow Brook event—a show recognized as one of America's finest concours and often mentioned in the same breath as the acclaimed gathering at Pebble Beach. Just looking at the contents of Smith's garage, collectors can be assured that Smith knows a thing or two about automobiles and the fine presentation thereof.

Smith owns cars that he likes, and some are what might be considered interesting but not necessarily amazing or significant. His pristine Sunbeam Tiger and Porsche 356 Cabriolet, both 1965 models, fit this description. They are

Above: Ferrari's little Dino has aged well. Its lines flow gracefully over the lightweight aluminum rims. The gold paint shows off the shape nicely, making Smith's 1972 example look quite sculptural.

Previous spread: Sitting like separate dollops of color on a painter's pallet, Smith's cars are finished in a great range of colors. Select pieces of automotive art and memorabilia decorate the walls.

sporty two-seat convertibles, but when set against Smith's 1972 Ferrari Dino or 1959 Alfa Romeo Sprint Speciale, the former seem like wallflowers. Smith purchased the Dino with the intent of repainting it. "At first I thought, 'A gold Ferrari, something's just wrong with that.' But then one day one of the guys at the shop and I wet sanded the paint to see how it would look, and it came back beautifully. Now I've decided I really love the color, and it's different from all the red and black ones you see."

Even more unusual than the Dino is the graceful Bertone-bodied Alfa Romeo Giulietta Sprint Speciale. Smith's is a rare pre-production prototype built with a long-nose body and no bumpers. The look is much cleaner than

the full production models, and according to several Alfa Romeo owner registries, only about a dozen are known to exist. Powered by a little 1,300cc engine (79 cubic inches) with only 91 horsepower, its styling is what satisfies owners, as its performance is leisurely.

Addressing Smith's need for speed is his 1967 Ferrari 275 GTB/4. Like all 275s, this one is powered by a legendary Colombo V-12, but Smith's features six two-barrel carburetors in place of the more common three three-barrel units. Adding to the Ferrari's rarity is that the engine is surrounded by a long-nose body designed by Pininfarina and produced by Scaglietti entirely out of aluminum. Track tests done in the day claimed the GTB/4 could hit

Two sports cars from 1965 sit tucked away in their tight quarters for the long Detroit winter. In the foreground is a Porsche 356 Cabriolet. Next to the German icon is another of Carroll Shelby's creations, a Sunbeam Tiger, an English sports car fitted with a small American V-8.

165 mph. Only six cars of this configuration were produced. Smith's is one of three with left-hand drive.

Delivering power in a decidedly different manner is Smith's dark green 1939 Lincoln Zephyr. Under its hood where a rather anemic V-12 once sat is a supercharged Chevrolet 454-cubic-inch V-8 producing approximately 650 horsepower. Smith cautions, "With this car, you'd better make sure that nobody's in front of you when you hammer it, because this thing just rips up the pavement."

Like the drivetrain, the interior of the Zephyr received a complete renovation. Modern conveniences were added, and unbeknownst to Smith, the craftsman responsible for the interior had Smith's young daughter in mind during the build. The Zephyr now features a sideways-facing rear seat complete with a safety belt and a DVD-player with monitor. Smith says, "It was a surprise to me that my interior guy was going to do this. But he knew my wife and daughter go everywhere with me, so he made sure we could all ride in the Zephyr when it was finished. My daughter loves it."

Even though the drivetrain and interior were modified during the car's restoration, Smith left the body alone.

Looking hungry, Smith's 1967 Shelby GT350 eyes his authentic 1966 Mini Cooper S. Smith notes, "As a family we use the Shelby a lot because it has a back seat, but by far, the Cooper S is the most fun to drive out of any car in the collection."

Very few long-nose Alfa Romeo Giulietta Sprint Speciales were produced in the late 1950s. Smith's is from 1959, and as a "prototype," the car was produced without bumpers, giving it an even cleaner look.

One of only nine produced, the 1936 Stout Scarab is an all-aluminum van-type creation featuring a rear-mounted Ford flathead V-8 and rear-drive. One can debate whether the vehicles' extraordinarily high price ($5,000) limited their appeal, or whether it was the ungainly styling or performance.

He believes the car's lines were drawn right to begin with. All that was changed on the outside was the removal of the bumpers (Smith, after all, does own a body shop) and the license plate holder—change that further uncluttered the car's already sweeping line. Now, when the car fires up, a vacuum-operated lever swings the license plate down from its retracted position under the rear bumper.

While not as elegant as the Zephyr, the designers behind Smith's dark blue 1939 Graham also knew something about style. Commonly referred to as a Shark Nose, this car was like an Edsel or Aztek in that the public quickly rejected the styling. Smith says, "That forward-leaning grille and the formed-in headlights are pure art deco. But people hated them, and since the cars were cheap anyway, when they were done with them they just threw them away." Being unloved, few Grahams survived, but today the marque is growing in popularity as collectors recognize the boldness of its styling.

With styling that is even wilder than the Graham, Smith's 1936 Stout Scarab is in a class of its own. Hailing from Dearborn, Michigan, William Stout was an aeronautical engineer who helped conceive of the Ford Tri-Motor. Stout also had intentions of revolutionizing automotive design, and his Scarab produced between 1935 and 1936 demonstrated his intentions. The aluminum body was lightweight. The engine and transaxle were mounted in a space-saving configuration in the rear. The roomy interior featured balsa wood paneled doors and a completely flat, carpeted floor. Passengers were supposed to sit in flimsy looking folding chairs that intentionally lacked permanent mounting points so that they could be placed in any configuration. A folding card table was also part of the interior package. While the Scarab's interior foreshadowed the reconfigurable 2008 minivans from Chrysler (available with a table and seats that rotate 180 degrees), Stout's design was

not without its faults. One can only imagine what would happen to the unrestrained occupants, chairs, and table if the Scarab's driver stopped suddenly during a card game.

Like all nine Scarabs produced, Smith's car was sold to a famous rich person, a French publishing magnate. The wealthy were the only ones who could afford the steep price of the Scarab, $5,000, a price equal to the luxurious Packards and Cadillacs of the day. As the story goes, the car spent most of its life in France, purportedly transporting Generals Eisenhower and de Gaulle at various points. Some years later, after it had apparently fallen into disrepair, the car was used by a circus to house monkeys until Philippe Charbonneaux, a French auto-

Smith's 1939 Lincoln Zephyr and 1967 Ferrari 275 GTB/4 are generations and worlds apart in terms of styling and technology. There's no mistaking their country of origin, and once their engines fire up, you can tell the American from the Italian just by their exhaust note.

Following cars like the Cord 812 and the Chrysler Airflow, the inexpensive Graham "Shark Nose" brought art deco styling to the masses. The only problem was that the masses didn't like it, and Grahams sold poorly. Smith rescued this example and appreciates its sculpted nose and integrated headlamps.

motive designer, bought it for his museum in the early 1960s.

When the aging Charbonneaux dispersed his collection in the late 1990s, Smith purchased the Stout. Restoring the primitive aluminum unibody was a major effort helped immeasurably by his company's experience repairing current aluminum-bodied Mercedes, BMWs, and Jaguars. Many interior pieces needed to be recreated from scratch, as Stout did not establish an official parts distribution network for his now 70-year-old Scarabs. Smith regularly shows the Scarab, and the vehicle is often on loan to museums around the globe.

Smiling with pride at his current collection, Smith concludes, "Going way, way back, I think you could say that it started because I was interested in cars in grade school. My parents were non-automotive, and as a matter of fact my mother didn't even have her driver's license until I was 14 or 15. And my dad always bought the cheapest Chevrolet he could . . . three on the tree with no options, that was just his way of buying cars. I probably got bit when I was 8 or 9, but my parents didn't believe in wasting money on buying car magazines, so that prompted me to work so that I could buy car magazines. I got my first car when I was 15, and the passion started to develop even further. In high school, I bought and sold a lot of Triumphs, and that came from working at a Triumph dealership on Detroit's East side. My junior and senior year in high school, I probably had a hand in selling 200 or 300 cars. This helped me pay for college, and I just kept working." The work, it seems, has paid off. ◆

Larry Smith is the chairman of the highly regarded Meadow Brook Concours d'Elegance but still finds time to run his business, Autometric Collision, perhaps the Midwest's most technically advanced collision repair facility.

This restored 1932 Ford is pretty tame as far as hot rods go. Smith's example survives with its roof at full height (not chopped) and a relatively stock flathead V-8 up front.

Chapter 17
CLASSICS AND MACKS

GARAGE OWNER: **PHIL BRAY**

Photography by Bobby Alcott

Ten thousand miles accrued on a 1911 Oldsmobile. Seventeen thousand miles rolled up on a 1914 Locomobile. Twenty-seven thousand miles driven in a 1940 Packard Darrin. Phil and Carol Bray drive their classics. Carol says quite matter of factly, "We have a garage queen every now and again, but we thoroughly enjoy the driving aspect of the hobby." Indeed.

Phil is yet another example of the talent and depth of knowledge that exist within Detroit's car community. He possesses skills far beyond those of manipulating antique steering gears, arcane spark advance levers, and archaic shifting mechanisms. After thirty years on the manufacturing side of the automotive business, Bray's knowledge of how to build things is considerable. For instance, say you need a working cylinder head for a 1914 Locomobile— Bray creates new heads from patterns he makes himself. The process is straightforward; Bray turns his patterns over to a local foundry for casting. The raw castings are then delivered to a local machine shop for finishing. With skills such as these, Bray gives life back to cars so old and so rare that the possibility of finding a new or usable used part has long since expired.

Phil completes most of the restorations at his home in Grosse Ile, Michigan, less than an hour south of Detroit. The couple purchased their home site in 1989 and completed construction the next year. Size tells the story. In addition to their 3,200 square feet of living space on the top floor, the ground level is a full workshop that equals the size of their living area. The workshop is accessed from the home's back side via four garage doors. Up one level on the side of the home is a second garage that is for clean storage and parking. It adds 1,600 square feet to the home.

A 1936 Mack Jr. awaits restoration in the lower level of Phil and Carol Bray's home in Grosse Ile, Michigan. The 3,200-square-foot workshop is large enough to store several vehicles while working on several others.

Previous spread: Twin double garage doors provide access to the clean storage and display space where eight classics are parked. A sharp eye will note a modern Chevrolet SSR convertible and 1928 Model A pickup, two more examples of Phil's current infatuation with pickups.

This once jaunty REO Flying Cloud Sedan from 1933 will be used as a "donor" car for the restoration of Bray's second Mack Jr. pickup. The vehicles are identical from the passenger compartment forward.

Carol says that most of her friends are understanding about the couple having more garage space than living space. She simply doesn't worry about those who don't get it.

Phil is a longtime collector and restorer and puts his considerable skills to good use. To hear Carol explain it, "Phil becomes obsessed with certain things. When we met, Phil was obsessed with Packards. Then he moved on to Marmons, and now he's moved on to pickups." Pickups? Phil, in his own words, explains, "The first one of these I saw was thirty-five years ago in Montgomery, Alabama, and I said, 'Boy, is that a neat-looking pickup truck. I'm gonna get one of those.' It took me thirty-three years to find one because they only made two hundred of them, and now there aren't that many left."

The truck Phil Bray speaks of is a 1936 Mack Jr. Produced only for two years (1936 and 1937). This stylish truck came about by accident. The REO company, one of Ransom Eli Oldsmobile's ventures, had extra bodies left-over from a run of 1933 REO Flying Cloud Sedans. As records proved, REO purchased 2,000 bodies from a Michigan producer, but only used 1,300 of them. The remaining bodies weren't much use to REO at the time, as its 1934 Flying Cloud Sedan was updated from the 1933 design.

Faced with the question of what to do with 700 perfectly good car bodies, REO decided to convert them to half-ton pickups. This wasn't a stretch decision for REO, as the company already had a 30-year history in the truck business. Two nearly identical models were produced, one wearing REO badging, and the other (only 200 units) were produced for the Mack Truck company. The Macks were sold under the name Mack Jr. and featured the brand's bulldog mascot as a hood ornament.

Thinking that he'd never find one of the 200 Mack Jr.s produced, the Brays settled on a 1936 REO pickup and restored it. Carol says, "Once you start working on a rare car, you begin developing a network of people who are interested in the same kind of car. You share

Phil and Carol Bray enjoy the driving aspect of the automotive hobby. Together, they've driven their antique cars more than 50,000 miles in road rallies, caravans, and transcontinental events.

This 1911 Oldsmobile race car was originally owned by a playboy from Boston who raced the car extensively. Powered by a massive 500-cubic-inch four-cylinder, it is capable of more than 85 mph.

A diamond among rubies, the Bray's 1932 Chrysler Imperial CL is a national award winner at classic car shows. One of only 20 produced in 1932, few remain, but its rarity won't keep this classic safe in a garage. In May 2007, the car participated in a ten-day caravan throughout the American SouthWest.

information and sources of parts. And it just keeps on growing." Not long after the REO project was under-way, Phil learned of a Mack Jr. in Washington state. It took Phil more than two years to cajole the truck's owner into selling, but he did, and the rest is history in the remaking.

Phil estimates that there are only a handful of the Macks left, and now he owns two, finding the second one in Indiana. One is now perfect and the other is in the midst of a complete restoration in the lower level of the Brays' home. Related to these two Mack Jr.s, the Brays also own a 1933 REO Flying Cloud Sedan that he's using as a parts car for the "project" Mack Jr.

These trucks stand out in sharp contrast to Bray's brass-era and more traditional classic cars. The oldest

This 1935 Pierce Arrow cuts a classic profile, with sweeping lines running along the fenders and tapered roof. This example is particularly handsome because of the rear-mounted spare-tire carrier. This mounting location leaves the fenders completely smooth and clean.

With a special body designed by Howard "Red" Darrin, this 1940 Packard is one of the Brays' favorite drivers. It's been across the country several times and even traveled to Alaska.

vehicle in Bray's collection is his 1911 Oldsmobile racer. According to the two years of research Phil and Carol put into their Oldsmobile, the car originally carried an open speedster body. The first owner, a playboy named Greenway Albert, discarded the original for the racing body now on the car. In this form, it saw extensive track competition, and was kept by Albert until his death in the 1960s.

While most cars of this vintage continue to age peacefully separated from the world by velvet ropes in a climate-controlled museum, the Brays have cruised more than 10,000 miles in their Oldsmobile. Phil says, "This thing is just a blast to drive." While he is talking, he fires the Oldsmobile's massive 500-cubic-inch four cylinder—that's more than 8 liters. Each cylinder is five inches round and has a stroke of half a foot. While the old beast idles cleanly with a rather raspy yet powerful exhaust note, Phil continues, "She'll run 85 miles per hour easy. I've done a couple of things to make her more reliable, such as full-pressure oiling, a high-compression cylinder head, and adding hydraulic brakes."

Rolling on wood wheels, the Brays have driven their 1914 Locomobile touring car more than 17,000 miles. Significantly over engineered, the Locomobile is reliable, powerful, and enormous. Exposing his extensive background in manufacturing, Bray is casting completely new cylinder heads for himself and other Locomobile owners.

A fully modern Chevrolet SSR shares space with antique pickups in the Brays' "display garage." Dwarfed by the massive Locomobile, Bray built a Volkswagen Beetle Speedster to win a bet over a steak dinner.

Carol chimes in, "Phil doesn't like cars that don't perform. And we treat them like real cars."

The Brays have put even more miles on their 1914 Locomobile. Because of its advanced engineering and sheer opulence, the Locomobile was often thought of as America's Rolls Royce. Fitting this descriptor, in 1914 Bray's touring car would have cost more than $6,000, the 2007 equivalent of $120,000. The Locomobile's six-cylinder is sized appropriately to its original sale price, displacing 525 cubic inches. Like so many of the world's most remarkable early cars, the Locomobile's engine offers a retrospective glimpse into the future. Each of its

cylinders utilizes two spark plugs—a feature now found in current high-performance engines, including some powering Porsches.

Along with a stunning 1935 Pierce Arrow Rumble Seat Coupe, the Brays also enjoy their rare 1932 Chrysler Imperial CL. The couple did a complete restoration on the car several years back, and have won regional and national awards with it. But like their other cars, the Chrysler was engineered to be a wonderful driving machine. In May 2007, the car participated in a 10-day caravan driving event throughout the American Southwest.

Another driver is Bray's stunning 1940 Packard Darrin. Howard "Red" Darrin was an independent designer who penned coach-work in Europe prior to World War II. He came to the United States in the early 1930s, settled in Los Angeles, and started his American career designing cars for the stars. In 1937, Darrin built his first Packard for Clark Gable. In 1938, Darrin built five more, many of which also went to Hollywood types. The Brays' example was begun in Darrin's Los Angeles factory, but was then shipped to the company's new production facility in Indiana for completion.

Phil acquired the car, restored it to a very high standard, won many awards with it, and then put it on the road. Phil says, "Just a couple summers ago we drove the car to Alaska. Forty-seven hundred miles in all. Since its restoration, I think we're up to twenty-seven thousand miles. But I've done a little to it, including twin carburetors and a high-compression head. With the overdrive, it will do close to 100 miles per hour."

In talking with the Brays, it's obvious they enjoy being keepers of history in both tangible and intangible ways. Their collection spans decades, but more important, their collection is living out its life on the road, right where it belongs. ◆

Chapter 18
FLATHEADS AND FLAME JOBS

GARAGE OWNER: **BOB ADAMS**

Photography by Bobby Alcott

Hot rod progenitors were young bucks. Imagine them, just back from World War II. These men, part of what has been called the Greatest Generation, were used to risk and excitement. Cut from this unique bolt of cloth, many of these men developed one of the most influential and purely American genres of the automotive world: the hot rod.

Because of their powerful draw, it's not uncommon for hot rods to attract people far younger than those who started the trend. Bob Adams is one of those younger guys. A Boomer, Adams didn't grow up around the dry lakebeds of California or next door to guys building land-speed record cars made out of discarded aeronautical fuel tanks. Woodward Avenue during the height of the muscle car boom was Adams' playground. But it was hot rods that eventually captured Adams' imagination, and then everything else about him.

By day, Adams is an executive at Crain Communications, a multi-national publishing and communications company based in Detroit. (Titles such as *AutoWeek, Automotive News*, and *Advertising Age* are part of Crain.) Adams has been with the firm for decades, and when he's not working, he's in his two-level garage in Orion, Michigan.

The structure, built in 2000, works with the topography of his residential parcel, the upper floor accessed from the top of Adams' hill facing south, and the lower section opening to the west at the lot's lowest point. Overall, the top floor measures out to 42 feet wide by 65 feet deep. The lower section (built into the hill) is the same width but only half as deep. A space without windows, the bottom level is for storage only. Our visit came in the early spring; two of Adams' cars were still in hibernation down below:

The upper floor of Bob Adams' garage is almost 3,000 square feet of hot rod heaven. The display space doubles as work space and cleans up pretty well to host parties for Adams' hobby friends.

Previous spread: Looking at one of Bob Adam's displays, it's impossible to deny the visceral appeal of the classic American hot rod.

a 1962 Amphicar (a combination car/boat made in Germany) and a 1964 Chevrolet Impala 409 Convertible.

During our time at his garage, Adams was preparing his hot rods for one of the largest and most prestigious indoor car shows in the country, the annual Detroit AutoRama. Adams' collection is now heavily skewed toward hot rods, but it wasn't always so. Adams explains how he first got into cars, and his story is familiar to so many in Detroit, "My family lived in Royal Oak, and my dad was an engineer for Chrysler Corporation. I grew up in the '60s, and I was just so into cars. When I was only 15, my friend and I made an illegal purchase. Anybody could buy a car back in those days. We pooled 50 bucks and bought a '54 Ford, a two-door post car. Our parents didn't know we had the car, and we kept it that way all summer, parking it on streets a few blocks away from either of our houses. We weren't even old enough to have

licenses back then, and we never titled or insured the car. We 'borrowed' plates so we could drive it, and we used to cruise Woodward. That was the scene we wanted to be part of."

As soon as Adams reached legal driving age, the Ford got sold, and with money saved from odd jobs and two paper routes, Adams bought a 1957 Oldsmobile with a Rocket V-8 engine. He remembers, "I really wanted something that had some performance. Muscle was everything, and at least the car had the V-8." The Olds didn't last long, and in 1966 a family friend helped find young Adams his first true muscle car. It was a 1962 Plymouth Fury with a 361 Golden Commando wedge motor hooked to a TorqueFlite three-speed automatic transmission. Adams remembers, "I jacked it up and put lights in the rear wheel wells to show off when I used to cruise through the drive-in parking lots. I got a few tickets in that car."

From there, Adams graduated to another Chrysler, a second-generation Plymouth Barracuda outfitted with the Formula S package and a 340-cubic-inch V-8. His tastes matured with age and the depth of his wallet. He moved into a phase of owning Corvettes and older Chevrolets.

His collection has gotten older and bigger since the late 1980s when he built his first hot rod. Today, that original car is gone, replaced several times over by a variety of hot rods that touch on several different categories within this broad classification. As one would expect in a collection of hot rods, there are those festooned with flames and powered by mighty flathead Ford V-8s.

Representing a recent movement that celebrates the roots of hot rodding is what Adams calls his Rat Rod. To him, and others who have rediscovered the rougher side of hot rods, these cars recall a more accurate representation of what mainstream hot rodding was like in the 1950s. Young guys would find a rough, but otherwise solid V-8-style Ford and soup it up. Money went to the drivetrain and chassis, not cosmetics.

Adams' garage is a two-story affair. The lower section is for vehicle storage only, while the upper story serves as a combination work space and retreat. The center opening of the lower level makes good use of Adams' rolling lot.

When he's around his hot rods, Bob Adams is a content guy and an easy smile comes across his face. An executive at Crain Communications, Adams has a hand in producing influential automotive publications. Pictured is a 1934 Ford Cabriolet with a supercharged Chevy small block.

The desired finish is a blend of oxidized paint and steel. Adams' anti-establishment Rat Rod rolls proudly in the face of hot rod convention by being exactly what it is, an original hot rod built in the 1950s when it was cooler to go fast than look good. The engine is a 330-cid Cadillac, a V-8 known for its power. The lever-system steering that runs on the exterior of the body was most likely transplanted from an old dirt track race car.

Proudly wearing an uneven coat of oxidized paint, a bit of rust, dull chrome, and weathered fabrics, Adams believes his to be an "original" Rat Rod—one that was actually built in the 1950s. The body is that of an original 1932 Ford, the first year of the Ford's famous V-8. The person (or people) who previously owned the car added many of the high-performance pieces that characterize the era, including period-correct big front drum brakes from a 1950s-era Buick, the Schroeder racing-style steering box, and a stout 330-cubic-inch Cadillac V-8. The Caddy's motor is topped with four "deuces" (two-barrel

Details that fit the imagined owner of the Rat Rod make the interior especially interesting. Careful observers will spy brass knuckles and presidential campaign mementos; note that the floorboards are partially formed out of an old steel Coke sign.

It's easy to spot Adams coming down the road in his lowered 1948 Chevy. It's a low-maintenance hot rod, meaning that while the paint and interior are customized, the car's suspension and running gear are not, so it's OK to get them dirty and leave them that way.

Adams drove this car home from California on Route 66 just a month after he bought it. The custom-built car is quite modern with features such as air conditioning, a high-powered audio system, and up-to-date safety equipment.

Streamlined for speed, Adams' 1927 Ford Model A is as clean as the Rat Rod is dirty. The narrow hood covers a modern Ford 2.3-liter four-cylinder. A four-bar suspension is used front and rear, directing tractor tires in front and grippy slicks in the rear.

Prepped for Detroit's AutoRama, this mostly stock 1939 Ford looks pretty mean with engine parts polished up and its hood removed. During our visit, the car occupied the space on Adams' hoist, another important dream garage feature.

carburetors). The car looks like it lost its fenders. Adams informs, "In the old days, they'd pull the fenders off to make the car lighter for when they raced it. Then, the next day when they'd have to go back to work and be 'respectable,' they'd put the fenders back on."

Adams particularly likes the car. It's easy to own and doesn't require any primping to keep it clean. Plus he and his wife, Gina, have taken it to many Rat Rod shows, events sometimes called "non-billet" events because no fancy aluminum parts are allowed.

While far from being Rat Rods, Adams owns another couple of hot rods that he calls "low-maintenance" drivers. One is his 1948 Chevrolet Truck. Sitting low thanks to a front subframe from a late-model Chevrolet Camaro, the rounded truck possesses an aggressive stance. A mildly built Chevrolet 350-cubic-inch V-8 provides the backup for the look, while the GM 700-R4 Hydramatic automatic transmission makes the truck easy to drive and a good highway cruiser because of its integral overdrive gear. Adams has done much of the work himself, including adding a heater, cruise control, and re-trimming much of the interior. Adams' attention to detail is shown in the truck's door logo, an Adams original right down to the postal zone code (the forerunner of today's ZIP code).

The second "driver" is a car he purchased at the Los Angeles Roadster Show, an event he attends with a group of friends every year. He explains, "We usually rent a transporter to ship our cars out there and spend the week bombing around L.A. in our hot rods. I hadn't planned on buying the car, so when it came time to leave and ship the cars home, the transporter was full, so I had to leave it behind." Later in the year, in the middle of the summer, he and Gina flew out to drive the car from L.A. back to Detroit. To keep things interesting, they drove on as much of the original Route 66 as possible.

The red 1932 Ford is not a restoration, but a purpose-built hot rod, built up from individually purchased components designed expressly for the huge hot rod market. Adams explains how the business of hot rods works, "It would really be a shame to customize an original older car that could be restored. Hot rods are almost always built from the ground up with newly produced parts. They get pieced together with the frame made by one company and body panels from another. Lots of hot rods don't have a single old piece in them."

A typical 350-cid Chevy fitted with a four-barrel carburetor moves the red '32 much more like a new muscle car than an antique. With gear such as air conditioning, an integrated heater, a large trunk, and equipment that enables the car to pass the National Street Rod Association's 32-point safety inspection, the Ford is a fairly practical street car. Adams even installed a third, high-mounted brake light. As drivable as it is, one thing is for sure, you'd never lose it in a parking lot. Adams says, "This is the one we can jump in and go anytime, anywhere."

Adams' other cars are what he calls high maintenance, "When I take these out, it takes hours to detail them to get them clean again." One look at Adams' low-slung 1927 Model A Roadster helps you understand his point. Virtually everything is perfectly finished in flawless paint or rich chrome, including suspension and steering components. This particular car was built in the early 1980s and showcases the work of many craftsmen native to Detroit. From the windshield forward, all of the body panels are hand-formed steel. That windshield is actually from a 1939 Garwood speedboat. In the style of the high-speed cars, the wide rear tires are slicks and the narrow front tires were originally intended for a farm tractor.

Like most current hot rods, this 1932 Ford is made from mostly new parts. The frames and suspension pieces are off-the-shelf parts produced just for this type of application. The Ford flathead V-8 started the hot rod movement. This particular mill is from 1953 and has received a serious injection of power. The induction system uses three two-barrel carburetors. A modern five-speed manual transmission backs up the engine and directs power rearward to a quick-change Halibrand rear end.

The interior of Adams' 1932 Ford roadster features many restored pieces from an original 1932 Ford. The dashboard and instrumentation provide a powerful contrast to the chromed and modernized flathead V-8 that powers the car.

Looking ready to make a high-speed run on the salt flats of Bonneville, Utah, the number 75c 1932 Ford is owned by a friend of Adams. Adams was providing temporary storage for the car, which had been invited to a special display of 1932 Fords at the 2007 Detroit AutoRama.

The best hot rod builders know how to incorporate special details into their creations. The engine in the Bonneville car is chromed and polished in an expected manner, but detailing such as stripes in the air intakes shows extra effort and imagination.

Another high-maintenance car is Adams' black 1939 Ford Business Coupe. Every body panel on the car is stock, as is the interior. Fitted with an appropriate stock Ford flathead V-8, the only modifications are some polished parts and fancy cylinder heads. Adams was showing the Business Coupe at the 2007 Detroit AutoRama following our photo shoot, and he had the car prepped for a special look that he wanted. He explains, "I wanted it to look like a kid's hot rod, so we took off the hood so you could see the engine, then we dropped the front axle so it had a better stance. Then all we did was remove the hubcaps. The look with the painted wide lug wheels is really good—something you'd expect a kid to do who couldn't afford fancier chromed wheels."

As for the car that Adams likes best, he readily admits that it's a tough choice between his 1934 Ford Cabriolet and his sinister-looking 1932 Ford Roadster. The flame job paint scheme on the former was almost hot enough to melt the snow off of Adams' back lawn during our well-below-freezing photo shoot. The flow of colors and the movement of the flames is true art put into motion by a famous West Coast painter named Manual Reyes.

Equipped with a comfortable seating area that sports a refrigerator and a flat-screen TV, there's not much reason to ever leave Adams' garage. The antique jukebox is ready to drop the vinyl and provide tunes for yet another night of wrenching and polishing.

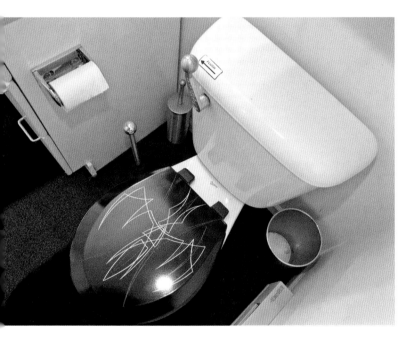

Even the washroom in Adams' garage received the hot rod treatment. Custom pinstriping decorates nearly every surface, and the flushing mechanism appears to have four gears worth of power. *Photo by Rex Roy*

Reyes was also responsible for the flame job on the Ford hot rod that starred alongside a young Martin Sheen in the 1974 made-for-TV movie, *The California Kid*. Adams' rod, easily the fastest in his collection, would probably make short work of Sheen's car thanks to the high-performance ZZ4 crate engine from GM Performance Parts. In normal trim the engine produces nearly 400 horsepower, but Adams added a centrifugal supercharger and a pair of four-barrel carburetors, significantly increasing the engine's output.

The latter roadster is what Adams calls "1:00 a.m. Blue," a color so dark that it only appears blue in direct sunlight. This all-steel car features a number of carefully crafted details that separate it from run-of-the-mill cars. Aside from the exquisitely detailed engine, the interior gets high marks for its classy execution. The tucked and rolled upholstery wraps around the driver and passenger, placing them directly in front of a beautifully restored 1932 dashboard and instrument cluster. Adding to the originality of the interior is the period-correct steering wheel and shifter.

While there are more expensive cars to be owned and larger collections to be had, Bob Adams is content with himself and his hot rods. Even his wife loves the action and the people that comprise the hobby. The couple is currently building a hot rod for her that is themed off of the legendary Ford Mustang. Every couple should be so happy. ◆

Chapter 19
THE ENGINEER'S WORKSHOP

GARAGE OWNER: **JIM DUNHAM**

Driving on the back roads of Plymouth, Michigan, it's normal to see homes with large outbuildings. Barns, too, are still common in this not-quite-fully-suburban community about a 45-minute drive from Detroit. But the content of Jim Dunham's side-entrance barn is far from agricultural. This 20-plus-year veteran of Ford Motor Company works on automotive projects of dizzying complexity within his tidy, wood-sided structure.

Walking into Jim's dream garage, it's difficult to know where to look first. Every square inch of space is occupied by serious-looking machinery. Beside all manner of metal-working devices (an English wheel, wood hand-forming tools, and a slip roller), there are Porsches, an enormous low-slung tube frame, and what looks to be parts of a Ford GT40 made out of steel and wood. Wood?

The tube frame, in fact, is the beginning of a Porsche 917 race car, one of the most famous racers to ever hail from Stuttgart. With a matter-of-fact attitude, Dunham waves off the Porsche frame as if any child could build the exact same thing from an Erector Set. As though he were explaining how to sharpen a lawn mower blade, Dunham says, "The quarter scale plans I was given weren't too detailed, but it was enough to give me the geometry, and that's all I need to build a car. I just laid it out and did XYZ coordinates of each point, and then put that into a CAD program. That gives you all of your nodal points, and then you're ready to go." With such well-developed engineering and CAD skills, Dunham's frame will one day carry a completed 917 into vintage racing competition. (A note to all aspiring car constructors: the same drawings Dunham started with can be purchased off the Internet for about 10 bucks.)

Above: Located on the outskirts of Plymouth, Michigan, Dunham's barn blends in with the agricultural roots of the area. Many homes and farms in the area still have outbuildings, but none contain treasures the likes of Dunham's.

Previous spread: Looking down from his storage area, it's apparent that Jim Dunham's barn provides ample room for building cars from the ground up. The large worktable is actually a homebuilt surface plate, a perfectly flat surface used to build chassis with pinpoint accuracy.

While impressive, the complexity of Dunham's two other major projects dwarf the 917 build. Both projects center on Ford's legendary GT40, a car that Dunham has long admired. His admiration turned to dreams of owning one, but cost and practicality are the twin spoilers of such dreams. These barriers, however, weren't nearly tall enough to discourage this 6-foot 7-inch Detroiter. When faced with the reality that he'd never be able to afford an

original Ford GT40 on his engineer's salary, he decided to simply build one. After all, as an engineer at Ford, he knew every step necessary to bring a car to life.

Ambling his towering frame toward the design buck he built, Dunham explains, "In 1997, I kicked off the idea of building my own GT40, an accurate replica of a 1965 Mark I." The Mark Is were short-tail models with small-block V-8 engines, a design so iconic that Ford essentially

What happens when an engineer dreams about owning a car he can't afford? In Detroit, he simply builds one from scratch. This wooden creation is called a design buck, and it enables engineers to make the pieces of their automotive puzzle fit together. Dunham built this buck from plans he drew up on his own.

Dunham's hand-fabricated design buck sits in the foreground foreshadowing the 1965 Ford GT40 Mark I he would build. The nearly completed car sits in the paint booth that is integrated into Dunham's garage. The major work is complete, and the car awaits final engineering and trim details.

An exciting detail of Dunham's own GT40 is the multi-carburetor setup that tops the rear-mounted high-performance 302-cubic-inch V-8. In a lucky turn of fate, Dunham was able to locate a used GT40 gearbox and transaxle to complete the project.

Looking through a labyrinth of monocoque and aluminum tubing, Dunham contemplates his next move by studying plans he developed by reverse-engineering original Ford GT40s.

Looking like a birdcage, this frame for a Porsche 917 race car was built by Dunham from nothing more than 1/4-scale drawings. The monocoque of an original 1966 Ford GT40 sits in the background. Dunham's plans are laid out in the foreground on his homemade surface plate.

reincarnated that exact model for the Ford GT that was introduced in 2003. Dunham methodically continues, "In order to start the build I had to get drawings, but I wasn't able to find original blueprints. So I went around finding original GT40s to measure and photograph. Then I made technical drawings of these by hand. That took me about two years. Then I converted them to CAD." One of the cars Dunham visited most often was the GT40 that Ford donated to the Indianapolis Motor Speedway Museum after the company's 1966 sweep of the French endurance classic, 24 Hours of Le Mans. This particular GT, while not one of the podium finishers at Le Mans, was a Mark II—a model with a significant racing pedigree. The museum

staff allowed Dunham to partially disassemble the car to facilitate his documentation.

With plans completed, Dunham says, "I built a design-aid buck. This let me get the basic geometries right even for the toughest part, which is the roof with all of the compound curves and the intersection of the windshield and doors." Dunham explains the process as if any regular Joe could do the same thing in his own garage.

Showing the level of resourcefulness so typical among Detroit car guys and Motor City engineers, Dunham made his own body panels. He procured an original GT40 body from England and used it to make molds. From these, he replicated the hood, deck, and

Awaiting restoration, the doors and hood from GT40 chassis #1032 are stacked in the paint booth of Dunham's garage barn. In addition to the paint booth, Dunham's barn includes an engine-build room and mezzanine storage.

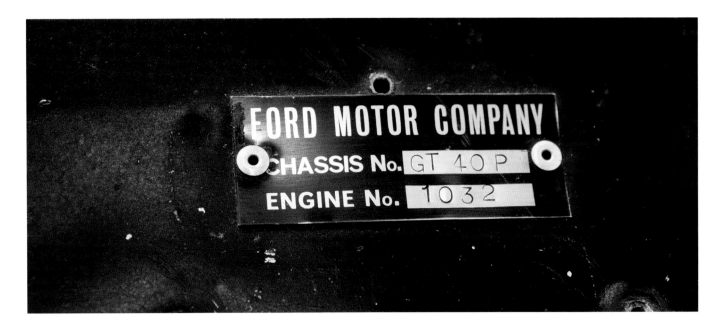

This vehicle identification number tag makes the original 1966 Ford GT40 in Dunham's barn worth a small fortune. Chassis 1032 raced at Sebring and Le Mans and was donated to the Indianapolis Motor Speedway Museum by Ford, where it remained until Dunham and a team of Ford engineers began its restoration on behalf of the museum.

The bare block is an original Ford 427-cubic-inch "side oiler," the same type used in 1966 GT40 Mark II models. The mounting point for the oil pump can be seen on the side of the block toward the left side of the photo.

fenders. Original, reproduction, and aftermarket parts were used to complete the balance of body, chassis, and suspension. Dunham slightly modified the interior to suit his tall build, but the interior has a period look and feel, as does the multi-carbed, 302-cubic-inch V-8. The windshield is produced by a company in South Africa.

Dunham's own GT40 was nearing completion during our visit, but his second GT40 project was just beginning, and necessitated moving his own car to the back burner. In an interesting twist of fate, the same GT40 Mark II Dunham studied so carefully to recreate his own car is now also in his Plymouth garage.

Helping lead a team of Ford engineers who are donating their time and sweat, the GT40 is being restored for the Indianapolis Motor Speedway Museum.

Dunham says, "The goal of our restoration is to get the car running again. When Ford donated the car to the museum in 1969, they took the running engine out and put an old, blown-up NASCAR engine in it. We've already located a correct 427 side-oiler for it, and the same man who tuned the engine for *this* car in 1966 at Le Mans is rebuilding its engine today." The man he's referring to is Moses Nolan, a 50-plus-year veteran at Ford and a living legend at Ford Motorsports. Dunham continues, "By the end of 2007, this will be a running car that will be capable of parade laps and demonstration runs at Indy. And when people hear that 427, it will be great. The sound is just deafening."

The specific history of this GT40, chassis number 1032, includes taking second place at Sebring in 1966 with pilots

This is one Porsche you'll see coming. Once just a stock 1972 911, Dunham completely refurbished the car and equipped it to become a race-ready RSR edition. Dunham maintains a competition license, and his Porsches see wheel-to-wheel action on a regular basis.

Looking across the reinforced engine compartment of the race-prepared Porsche 914-6 that he built with friends in 1989, Dunham's completely stock 1972 Porsche 911-T sees frequent summer-time use.

Mark Donahue and Walt Hansgen at the wheel. For that race, the car wore white paint and the number 3. Repainted a gold-toned color called Amber Glow and wearing number 4, the car also competed at Le Mans. Ford GT40s swept the race 1-2-3 in 1966, but chassis 1032 retired early with a failed clutch. After returning to the United States, Ford repainted the car for their victory tour, which explains how the car came to have its current black finish and number 2 on the doors. Dunham and company will finish the car in the same Amber Glow it wore at Le Mans.

If it weren't for the two GT40s and the Porsche 917 in the barn, Dunham's other cars would seem pretty special. Now relegated to wallflower status by comparison, Dunham loves his three 1972 Porsches. Two are fit for racing, the third is strictly for grocery duty. The fact that each is a 1972 model, Dunham claims, is pure coincidence. The striking yellow 911 is a near-perfect replica of the limited-edition lightweight,

race-ready RSR. Dunham is a licensed race driver, and competes often. His 914-6 is another track car, and yet another re-creation. The car was originally a garden-variety 914 fitted with a low-powered, four-cylinder engine. Dunham transplanted a high-powered, flat-six into the chassis to create the car pictured on these pages.

Dunham's third 1972 Porsche is the only stock vehicle in the barn. He found it used at a local Porsche dealer, and it was in such good condition, he just left it as he found it. He says, "It's just a cool little street car that you can jump in any time. The color is right and even though it's not very fast, it's still fun to drive."

Since he works for Ford in the advanced product group, one might think that Dunham would have his fill of cars. Obviously, such is not the case. And in Detroit, he's not the only man who brings his work home with him. ◆

Chapter 20
A GOOD PLACE

GARAGE OWNER: **KIP EWING**

Photography by Bobby Alcott

He exudes a perfect coolness—a Miles Davis kind of coolness—that few will ever obtain. Examples of his cool are legion, but most visible is the fact that Mattel produced a Hot Wheels scale model of a car this Detroiter conceived, engineered, and built.

It's good to be Kip Ewing.

With a sincere sense of gratitude, Ewing recognizes his fortunate station in life and the exciting steps he has taken to find himself where he is. Speaking purposefully in focused bursts, Ewing explains one of his latest projects while keeping up a conversation with his active three-year-old son, Lucas. This project was the unqualified hit of the 2005/2006 auto show circuit, the Ford GTX1. The GTX1 was born out of Ewing's desire to build a roadster version of the new-for-2003 Ford GT super car. Ewing says, "I ended up not being able to sell it as a production program from just sketches, so I took a 1/18th-scale model of a Ford GT and made it into a roadster. Then I put it on Hau Thai-Tang's desk. He liked what he saw."

Tang is the director of Ford's Advanced Product Creation and Special Vehicle Team. While he did not okay a full production program, Tang did give Ewing's topless concept an approval of sorts. Ford would provide one production GT to the private coachbuilder of Ewing's choosing. Working under Ewing's supervision, this coachbuilder would use its own resources to bring the GTX1 to life.

Ewing selected Mark Gerisch's shop in Green Bay, Wisconsin, for the project and his company, Genaddi Design Group, accepted the honor. Ewing recognized the craft Gerisch exhibited on past projects, specifically several current-generation Rolls Royce Phantoms. Ewing also knew that Genaddi could handle a production run of

Ewing's garage sports room for up to four cars plus plenty of tools. The tile floor is a heavy-duty variety that Ewing can weld on. The tile will retain its color even if paint stripper spills on it.

Previous spread: The clever observer might know an automotive designer lives at this house in Birmingham, Michigan. The home itself was built by and automotive designer , and it is now where Kip Ewing creates personal masterpieces.

Kip Ewing is currently an engineering supervisor on the Advanced Product Creation team at Ford Motor Company. The 2005 Ford GTX1 was Ewing's concept. While the concept did not win approval from Ford for full production, Ford did authorize a custom coachbuilder to build for-sale units. Genaddi Design Group of Green Bay, Wisconsin, handles the conversion for owners of 2003–2006 Ford GTs.

GT-X1

GTX1s if the market responded as expected. History would prove his thinking solid.

One might assume that chopping the top off of a Ford GT is no big deal, but such is not the case. The Ford GT is a complex, modern vehicle that utilizes a sophisticated aluminum monocoque. The project required extensive

The final stage of the GTX1's buildup occurred in Ewing's garage. Ewing handled many of the car's final details, including the sealing of the roadster's complex four-panel roof system. These snapshots were taken in the fall of 2005, just prior to the GTX1's debut. *Photos by Kip Ewing*

reengineering to maintain the GT's structural integrity. Gerisch could not have had a better project supervisor than Ewing, because this Detroiter was the official engineering supervisor on the 2003–2006 Ford GT. Literally, not figuratively, Ewing knows every nut, bolt, and weld in a GT.

Ewing's son, Lucas, was also involved in the project. When the lad was but 15 months old, his parents put him on the kitchen floor with four Ford GT models, each a color Ewing felt would work for the GTX1. Lucas picked the "lellow" one.

Gerisch's team performed most of the conversion in their Green Bay shop, but the final elements of the car's build were completed in Ewing's Bloomfield Hills, Michigan, garage. Ewing personally handled details such as the complex sealing necessary for the removable roof sections, as well as the final spit polishing before the presentation to Ford Motor Company executives in Dearborn, Michigan.

Once the GTX1 build was completed, Gerisch's company had invested approximately $350,000 in the conversion. Ewing's time and effort were not included in that figure, but his engineering contributions alone could be valued at half Gerisch's outlay. It's not easy or cheap to produce customized perfection that's capable of more than 200 miles per hour.

The finished GTX1 featured an innovative roof system comprised of four individual hard panels. The panels can be configured to provide a weatherproof closed coupe, a T-top, or a full convertible. Even with all of the panels in place, the outer panels can be locked into a vent position. Surprisingly for a vehicle with such limited cargo capacity as the GT, on-board storage is provided for the panels.

Completed on schedule for the 2005 industry extravaganza known as SEMA, the largest automotive aftermarket gathering in the world, the conversion stopped many of the 100,000 convention attendees in their tracks. So popular was the GTX1 that it became a requested show property for regional, national, and international auto shows. Further proof that Ewing's initial concept was an unqualified success, Gerisch's company had converted 45 Ford GTs into GTX1 models as of May 2007.

Ewing's personal history prepared him well for developing the GTX1. His schooling in mechanical engineering began at the University of Oklahoma in 1986. While still a

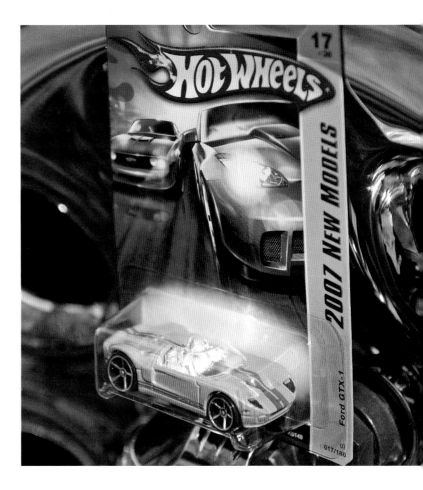

Mattel came out with this scale model of Ewing's GTX1 in 2007. While he's not a fan of the chrome interior, he sympathetically noted, "[Mattel] was probably looking for an easy way to add more flash to the design." *Photo by Rex Roy*

student, he restored cars for a private collector of Aston Martins, a job that would later lead to his interning for the hallowed marque as an engineer. This phase of life helps explain the stripped 1965 Aston Martin DBS in Ewing's garage. Ewing describes the car, "This is the very first DBS, it was the prototype. I love it because you can see the development process in the car so clearly. When something didn't work, the guys just changed it. Like, there wasn't enough legroom when they first built it, so they reconfigured the floor pan to move the front seats back and they changed the front footwell. My car wasn't even built with a functioning

Ewing has stripped the aluminum-bodied grand touring car down to its bare aluminum. Even missing most of its exterior, the aggressive lines of the DBS are unmistakably Aston Martin.

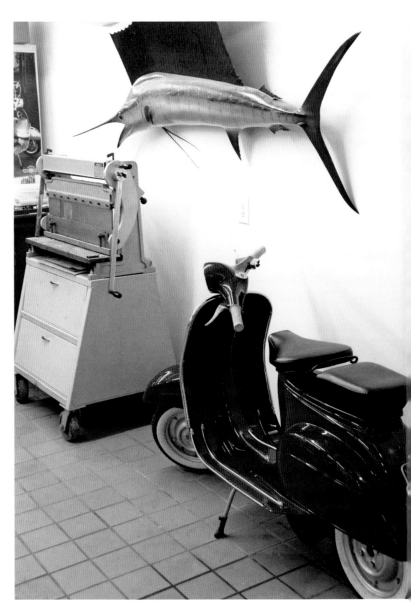

Ewing went through a phase of restoring Vespa scooters and ended up keeping one of the finished units for himself. Ewing keeps the sailfish because he just likes its look. He says, "One day I might put a hot-rod-style flame job on it."

HVAC system, so once they were finished with the car's structure, they just pop-riveted in ducting."

While the presence of the DBS is easy to explain, Ewing has a harder time explaining his 1985 Maserati Biturbo (pronounced "Bee-Turbo"). These diminutive sports cars were the Italian manufacturer's charge at BMW's popular 3-Series. While stylish, they were fragile and unreliable. Ewing purchased his low-mileage example when the previous owner dumped it after an engine fire. Sheepishly he explains, "The Maserati is a car that I've been working on for way too long. It's just turned into a bad case of 'while we're at it.' I originally bought it because the car had an engine fire, and I was just going to swap in a new powertrain. But once I finished putting in a 4.3 liter, I didn't like the way the car sat." After ditching the tiny Maserati 2.5-liter V-6 for the robust Chevrolet V-6, he lowered the car almost 3 inches. Wait, there's more. "It wasn't enough having the big engine and the lowered stance, so I start -

Ewing found a near-perfect 1985 Maserati Biturbo with a toasted engine. After performing an engine swap, his modifications continued with custom-made body panels he designed and manufactured himself.

ed modeling new body work for it," Ewing continues.

After months of effort, Ewing fashioned new front and rear fascias and rocker moldings, "I wanted to create pieces that continued on that 1980s sheer-form style. The goal was to have the car look like what Maserati would have built if they had stayed in the market to compete with a BMW M3. I wanted people to look at the car and say, 'Wow, that's a cool Biturbo, I've never seen one like that.' Not, 'Gee, look at all the stuff that's different.'" To Ewing, success comes when all the hard work that makes the car appear different melts away and can't be identified. Ewing made molds of his new body pieces out of gypsum cement, a cost-effective process that lets him make more than a dozen pieces from each mold.

Amazingly, most all of the work on these projects occurs right in Ewing's garage. The home was originally built in 1954 by another Detroit automotive personality, John Reinhardt. (Many enthusiasts will recognize one of Reinhardt's most notable designs, the classic Continental Mark II.) Built in the style of Frank Lloyd Wright, the home's design is timeless. At the end of a long drive, the double doors appear to access a standard two-car garage. Prior to Ewing's purchase of the home, a previous owner expanded the garage by making it a full car-length deeper, but Ewing discovered some issues: "The ceiling wasn't too stable, so I had to put in some extra beams. Plus I also needed flooring that I could strip paint and weld on. It was a lot of work, but the quarry tile floor I put down will take all kinds of abuse. You can drop an anvil on that floor and it won't crack. Plus I added heating and cooling, multiple outlets for 120 and 220 [volts], plus Cat-5 cabling to link computers from my home office to out here." Such a productive space allows projects to move in and out of this garage like letters from a postman's trolley.

All of this automotive fun is intertwined with a vibrant family life that clearly wasn't sacrificed at the altar of "The Career." This, perhaps, when all is said and done, is the most significant reason why it's good to be Kip Ewing. ◆

Looking down the side of Ewing's Biturbo, the massive six-cylinder from Ewing's 1965 Aston Martin DBS awaits reinstallation; it is the very first DBS ever produced.

Photo courtesy of Ford Motor Company

ACKNOWLEDGMENTS

Every project begins with a single action. Mine was to ring the Public Relations department at General Motors. I thought that I'd have a chance at making *Motor City Dream Garages* a reality if Bob Lutz would agree to show me his garage. A man I've known for over a decade returned my call. It was Dee Allen, the exemplar, consummate PR professional who handles GM's top brass. Because of Allen's efforts, Mr. Lutz graciously opened his collection, and *Motor City Dream Garages* had its start. Thank you, Dee.

From that point, completing the book became a matter of networking. Many of the garage owners, such as Greg Ornazian and Bill Couch, directed me to their friends. Other leads came from Wes Sherwood and Mark Shirmer at Ford Motor Company PR and William Stewart of the Walter P. Chrysler Museum. Gentlemen, thank you. The book is better because of your involvement.

Two additional people were crucial to the success of the book: lens man John Martin and ace shooter Bobby Alcott. Martin is a recognized talent in Detroit, but Alcott was new to the automotive image business. Alcott's work appears in nearly half of the book's chapters, and his skill at wielding his Nikon and Hasselblad speaks for itself at the rate of about 1,000 words per picture.

Last, I thank my family. My daughters, Hadley and Emma, were wonderful distractions, helping to keep balance in my life (plates of homemade cookies and miles of rollerblading) as I pounded out chapter after chapter. Even more important was my wife of 25 years who consistently and persistently supported the project with frequent encouragement, critical research, and insightful proofreading. While they never knew it, Tammy's effort significantly lightened the load of the professionals at MBI Publishing. Special thanks to you, Love. ◆

Final Words

"There is no cure for life or death, save enjoy the interval."
George Santayma

He who dies with the most toys wins.
Unknown

He who does with the most toys is still dead.
Unknown

"He who believes in me has everlasting life."
Jesus Christ, John 6:47

INDEX

Walking isn't a lost art; one must, by some means, get to the garage.

—Evan Esar